D1591118

THREE PLAYS

By Clifford Odets

AWAKE AND SING

WAITING FOR LEFTY

TILL THE DAY I DIE

Random House · PUBLISHERS

NEW YORK

For my Father and Mother

AWAKE

and

SING

NOTE

On the Original Presentation

THIS PLAY was first presented by the Group Theatre at the Belasco Theatre on the evening of February 19th, 1935, with the following members of the Group Theatre Acting Company:

	Played by
Myron Berger	ART SMITH
Bessie Berger	STELLA ADLER
Jacob	MORRIS CARNOVSKY
Hennie Berger	PHOEBE BRAND
Ralph Berger	JULES GARFIELD
Schlosser	ROMAN BOHNEN
Moe Axelrod	LUTHER ADLER
Uncle Morty	J. E. BROMBERG
Sam Feinschreiber	SANFORD MEISNER

The entire action takes place in an apartment in the Bronx.

The production was directed by HAROLD CLURMAN
The setting was designed by BORIS ARONSON

INTRODUCTION

By Harold Clurman

THE NAME OF CHEKHOV has been brought up in connection with "Awake and Sing!" The reference is flattering, of course, but perhaps a little misleading. For, while the American playwright does not especially cultivate his plot line, any more than the Russian, the whole quality of the former is active, impulsive and rather lusty, as compared to the thoughtful, delicately tempered and objective art of the man who wrote "The Cherry Orchard."

More Like Sean O'Casey

If comparisons are at all helpful in defining the nature of a playwright's talent, perhaps the name of Sean O'Casey may fit better in this connection. Not only do we find in "Awake and Sing!" some of the special tenement tenderness that lends warmth to all the cold facts of O'Casey's Dublin dramas, but there is also a certain quality of improvisatory spontaneousness, a tendency to give to all the occurrences that are part of the characters' lives the same importance and sympathy, whether they be intense suffering or workaday routine.

If we are disconcerted at first by such treatment, if it strikes us as too desultory or devil-may-care for good play-making, it is not only because we are used to more rigid patterns but because these playwrights are saying something through their plays that demands their special technique.

The lives of O'Casey's characters, like those in "Awake and Sing!" move on a level where it is almost impossible to differentiate between "high" and "low," "important" and "trivial," "essential" and "incidental." Thus in "Juno and the Pay-cock" as much time is given to Boyle's "musicales" as to the more vital aspects of his life or to the many woes that surround him. (And, indeed, are not Boyle's "inconsequential" activities part of the tragedy that is his life?)

So, in "Awake and Sing!" when the hapless son-in-law, whose wife has just told him that he is not the father of her child, says: "Look, I'm so nerv-ous! Twice I weighed myself on the subway," we have the same juxtaposition of the painful and the commonplace that calls forth deep laughter.

Poverty, or at least life-long economic pressure among city persons who still manage to get along "respectably," produces a certain lack of order, a confusion of physical details with spiritual crises which to the outside observer must appear just as laughable as it is saddening. Thus it is right in "Awake and Sing!" for Moe Axelrod to eat cake when he is told that he is losing the girl he loves, or to be angry because there are no oranges in the house while his heart is breaking.

The play is not "depressing," though some of

its incidents are harshly "true to life"; nor is it farcical, though some of its lines cause as much hilarity as vaudeville "gags." The play is about real people struggling humbly with their everyday problems; it is tragic in the sense that we are led to see that these problems are almost life-or-death matters; it is comic in the sense that the manner in which these problems present themselves for the characters in the play (and for most of us in the audience) is so amazingly casual and haphazard in relation to their fundamental significance.

H. C.

The Characters of THE PLAY

All of the characters in Awake and Sing! *share a fundamental activity: a struggle for life amidst petty conditions.*

BESSIE BERGER, *as she herself states, is not only the mother in this home but also the father. She is constantly arranging and taking care of her family. She loves life, likes to laugh, has great resourcefulness and enjoys living from day to day. A high degree of energy accounts for her quick exasperation at ineptitude. She is a shrewd judge of realistic qualities in people in the sense of being able to gauge quickly their effectiveness. In her eyes all of the people in the house are equal. She is naïve and quick in emotional response. She is afraid of utter poverty. She is proper according to her own standards, which are fairly close to those of most middle class families. She knows that when one lives in the jungle one must look out for the wild life.*

MYRON, *her husband, is a born follower. He would like to be a leader. He would like to make a million dollars. He is not sad or ever depressed. Life is an even sweet event to him, but the "old days" were sweeter yet. He has a dignified sense of himself. He likes people. He likes everything. But he is heartbroken without being aware of it.*

HENNIE *is a girl who has had few friends, male or female. She is proud of her body. She won't ask favors. She travels alone. She is fatalistic about being trapped, but will escape if possible. She is self-reliant in the best sense. Till the day she dies she will be faithful to a loved man. She inherits her mother's sense of humor and energy.*

RALPH *is a boy with a clean spirit. He wants to know, wants to learn. He is ardent, he is romantic, he is sensitive. He is naïve too. He is trying to find why so much dirt must be cleared away before it is possible to "get to first base."*

JACOB, *too, is trying to find a right path for himself and the others. He is aware of justice, of dignity. He is an observer of the others, compares their activities with his real and ideal sense of life. This produces a reflective nature. In this home he is a constant boarder. He is a sentimental idealist with no power to turn ideal to action.*

With physical facts—such as housework—he putters. But as a barber he demonstrates the flair of an artist. He is an old Jew with living eyes in his tired face.

UNCLE MORTY *is a successful American business man with five good senses. Something sinister comes out of the fact that the lives of others seldom touch him deeply. He holds to his own line of life. When he is generous he wants others to be aware of it. He is pleased by attention—a rich relative to the* BERGER *family. He is a shrewd judge of material values. He will die unmarried. Two and two make four, never five with him. He can blink in the sun for hours, a fat tomcat. Tickle him, he laughs. He lives in a pent house with a real Japanese butler to serve him. He sleeps with dress models, but not from his own showrooms. He plays cards for hours on end. He smokes expensive cigars. He sees every Mickey Mouse cartoon which appears. He is a 32-degree Mason. He is really deeply intolerant finally.*

MOE AXELROD *lost a leg in the war. He seldom forgets that fact. He has killed two men in extra-martial activity. He is mordant, bitter. Life has taught him a disbelief in everything, but he will fight his way through. He seldom shows his feelings: fights against his own sensitivity. He has been everywhere and seen everything. All he wants is* HENNIE. *He is very proud. He scorns the inability of others to make their way in life, but he likes people for whatever good qualities they possess. His passionate outbursts come from a strong but contained emotional mechanism.*

SAM FEINSCHREIBER *wants to find a home. He is a lonely man, a foreigner in a strange land, hypersensitive about this fact, conditioned by the humiliation of not making his way alone. He has a sense of others laughing at him. At night he gets up and sits alone in the dark. He hears acutely all the small sounds of life. He might have been a poet in another time and place. He approaches his wife as if he were always offering her a delicate flower. Life is a high chill wind weaving itself around his head.*

SCHLOSSER, *the janitor, is an overworked German whose wife ran away with another man and left him with a young daughter who in turn ran away and joined a burlesque show as chorus girl. The man suffers rheumatic pains. He has lost his identity twenty years before.*

The Scene of THE PLAY

Exposed on the stage are the dining room and adjoining front room of the BERGER *apartment. These two rooms are typically furnished. There is a curtain between them. A small door off the front room leads to* JACOB's *room. When his door is open one sees a picture of* SACCO *and* VANZETTI *on the wall and several shelves of books. Stage left of this door presents the entrance to the foyer hall of the apartment. The two other bedrooms of the apartment are off this hall, but not necessarily shown.*

Stage left of the dining room presents a swinging door which opens on the kitchen. (See frontispiece.)

Awake and sing, ye that dwell in dust:

ISAIAH—26:19

ACT · I

ACT · I

Scene
An Apartment in the Bronx.

Time
The Present; the family finishing supper.

RALPH: Where's advancement down the place? Work like crazy! Think they see it? You'd drop dead first.

MYRON: Never mind, son, merit never goes unrewarded. Teddy Roosevelt used to say——

HENNIE: It rewarded you—thirty years a haberdashery clerk!

JACOB *laughs.*

RALPH: All I want's a chance to get to first base!

HENNIE: That's all?

RALPH: Stuck down in that joint on Fourth Avenue—a stock clerk in a silk house! Just look at Eddie. I'm as good as he is—pulling in two-fifty a week for forty-eight minutes a day. A headliner, his name in all the papers.

JACOB: That's what you want, Ralphie? Your name in the paper?

RALPH: I wanna make up my own mind about things . . . be something! Didn't I want to take up tap dancing, too?

BESSIE: So take lessons. Who stopped you?

RALPH: On what?

BESSIE: On what? Save money.

RALPH: Sure, five dollars a week for expenses and the rest in the house. I can't save even for shoe laces.

BESSIE: You mean we shouldn't have food in the house, but you'll make a jig on the street corner?

RALPH: I mean something.

BESSIE: You also mean something when you studied on the drum, Mr. Smartie!

RALPH: I don't know. . . . Every other day to sit around with the blues and mud in your mouth.

MYRON: That's how it is—life is like that—a cake-walk.

RALPH: What's it get you?

HENNIE: A four-car funeral.

RALPHS What's it for?

JACOB: What's it for? If this life leads to a revolution it's a good life. Otherwise it's for nothing.

BESSIE: Never mind, Pop! Pass me the salt.

RALPH: It's crazy—all my life I want a pair of black and white shoes and can't get them. It's crazy!

BESSIE: In a minute I'll get up from the table. I can't take a bite in my mouth no more.

MYRON *restraining her:* Now, Momma, just don't excite yourself——

BESSIE: I'm so nervous I can't hold a knife in my hand.

MYRON: Is that a way to talk, Ralphie? Don't Momma work hard enough all day?

BESSIE *allows herself to be reseated.*

BESSIE: On my feet twenty-four hours?

MYRON: On her feet——

RALPH *jumps up:* What do I do—go to night-clubs with Greta Garbo? Then when I come home can't even have my own room? Sleep on a day-bed in the front room! *Choked, he exits to front room.*

BESSIE: He's starting up that stuff again. *Shouts to him:* When Hennie here marries you'll have her room—I should only live to see the day.

HENNIE: Me, too.

They settle down to serious eating.

MYRON: This morning the sink was full of ants. Where they come from I just don't know. I thought it was coffee grounds... and then they began moving.

BESSIE: You gave the dog eat?

JACOB: I gave the dog eat.

HENNIE *drops a knife and picks it up again.*

BESSIE: You got dropsy tonight.

HENNIE: Company's coming.

MYRON: You can buy a ticket for fifty cents and win fortunes. A man came in the store—it's the Irish Sweepstakes.

BESSIE: What?

MYRON: Like a raffle, only different. A man came in——

BESSIE: Who spends fifty-cent pieces for Irish

raffles. They threw out a family on Dawson Street today. All the furniture on the sidewalk. A fine old woman with gray hair.

JACOB: Come eat, Ralph.

MYRON: A butcher on Beck Street won eighty thousand dollars.

BESSIE: Eighty thousand dollars! You'll excuse my expression, you're bughouse!

MYRON: I seen it in the paper—on one ticket—765 Beck Street.

BESSIE: Impossible!

MYRON: He did . . . yes he did. He says he'll take his old mother to Europe . . . an Austrian——

HENNIE: Europe . . .

MYRON: Six per cent on eighty thousand—forty-eight hundred a year.

BESSIE: I'll give you money. Buy a ticket in Hennie's name. Say, you can't tell—lightning never struck us yet. If they win on Beck Street we could win on Longwood Avenue.

JACOB *ironically:* If it rained pearls—who would work?

BESSIE: Another county heard from.

RALPH *enters and silently seats himself.*

MYRON: I forgot, Beauty—Sam Feinschreiber sent you a present. Since I brought him for supper he just can't stop talking about you.

HENNIE: What's that "mockie" bothering about? Who needs him?

MYRON: He's a very lonely boy.

HENNIE: So I'll sit down and bust out crying " 'cause he's lonely."

BESSIE *opening candy:* He'd marry you one two three.

HENNIE: Too bad about him.

BESSIE *naïvely delighted:* Chocolate peanuts.

HENNIE: Loft's week-end special, two for thirty-nine.

BESSIE: You could think about it. It wouldn't hurt.

HENNIE *laughing:* To quote Moe Axelrod, "Don't make me laugh."

BESSIE: Never mind laughing. It's time you already had in your head a serious thought. A girl twenty-six don't grow younger. When I was your age it was already a big family with responsibilities.

HENNIE *laughing:* Maybe that's what ails you, Mom.

BESSIE: Don't you feel well?

HENNIE: 'Cause I'm laughing? I feel fine. It's just funny—that poor guy sending me presents 'cause he loves me.

BESSIE: I think it's very, very nice.

HENNIE: Sure . . . swell!

BESSIE: Mrs. Marcus' Rose is engaged to a Brooklyn boy, a dentist. He came in his car today. A little dope should get such a boy.

Finished with the meal, BESSIE, MYRON *and* JACOB *rise. Both* HENNIE *and* RALPH *sit silently at the table, he eating. Suddenly she rises.*

HENNIE: Tell you what, mom. I saved for a new dress, but I'll take you and Pop to the Franklin. Don't need a dress. From now on I'm planning to stay in nights. Hold everything!

BESSIE: What's the matter—a bedbug bit you suddenly?

HENNIE: It's a good bill—Belle Baker. Maybe she'll sing "Eli, Eli."

BESSIE: We was going to a movie.

HENNIE: Forget it. Let's go.

MYRON: I see in the papers—*as he picks his teeth*—Sophie Tucker took off twenty-six pounds. Fearful business with Japan.

HENNIE: Write a book, Pop! Come on, we'll go early for good seats.

MYRON: Moe said you had a date with him for tonight.

BESSIE: Axelrod?

HENNIE: I told him no, but he don't believe it. I'll tell him no for the next hundred years, too.

MYRON: Don't break appointments, Beauty, and hurt people's feelings.

BESSIE *exits.*

HENNIE: His hands got free wheeling. *She exits.*

MYRON: I don't know . . . people ain't the same. N-O- The whole world's changing right under our eyes. Presto! No manners. Like the great Italian lover in the movies. What was his name? The Sheik. . . . No one remembers? *Exits, shaking his head.*

RALPH *unmoving at the table:* Jake. . . .

JACOB: Noo?

RALPH: I can't stand it.

JACOB: There's an expression—"strong as iron you must be."

RALPH: It's a cockeyed world.

JACOB: Boys like you could fix it some day. Look on the world, not on yourself so much. Every country with starving millions, no? In Germany and Poland a Jew couldn't walk in the street. Everybody hates, nobody loves.

RALPH: I don't get all that.

JACOB: For years, I watched you grow up. Wait! You'll graduate from my university.

The others enter, dressed.

MYRON *lighting:* Good cigars now for a nickel.

BESSIE *to* JACOB: After take Tootsie on the roof. (*To* RALPH): What'll you do?

RALPH: Don't know.

BESSIE: You'll see the boys around the block?

RALPH: I'll stay home every night!

MYRON: Momma don't mean for you——

RALPH: I'm flying to Hollywood by plane, that's what I'm doing. *Doorbell rings.* MYRON *answers it.*

BESSIE: I don't like my boy to be seen with those tramps on the corner.

MYRON *without:* Schlosser's here, Momma, with the garbage can.

29

BESSIE: Come in here, Schlosser. *Sotto voce:* Wait, I'll give him a piece of my mind. MYRON *ushers in* SCHLOSSER *who carries a garbage can in each hand.* What's the matter the dumbwaiter's broken again?

SCHLOSSER: Mr. Wimmer sends new ropes next week. I got a sore arm.

BESSIE: He should live so long your Mr. Wimmer. For seven years already he's sending new ropes. No dumbwaiter, no hot water, no steam—— In a respectable house, they don't allow such conditions.

SCHLOSSER: In a decent house dogs are not running to make dirty the hallway.

BESSIE: Tootsie's making dirty? Our Tootsie's making dirty in the hall?

SCHLOSSER *to* JACOB: I tell you yesterday again. You must not leave her——

BESSIE *indignantly:* Excuse me! Please don't yell on an old man. He's got more brains in his finger than you got—I don't know where. Did you ever see—he should talk to you an old man?

MYRON: Awful.

BESSIE: From now on we don't walk up the stairs no more. You keep it so clean we'll fly in the windows.

SCHLOSSER: I speak to Mr. Wimmer.

BESSIE: Speak! Speak. Tootsie walks behind me like a lady any time, any place. So good-by... good-by, Mr. Schlosser.

SCHLOSSER: I tell you dot—I verk verry hard here. My arms is. . . . *Exits in confusion.*

BESSIE: Tootsie should lay all day in the kitchen maybe. Give him back if he yells on you. What's funny?

JACOB *laughing:* Nothing.

BESSIE: Come. *Exits.*

JACOB: Hennie, take care. . . .

HENNIE: Sure.

JACOB: Bye-bye.

HENNIE *exits.* MYRON *pops head back in door.*

MYRON: Valentino! That's the one! *He exits.*

RALPH: I never in my life even had a birthday party. Every time I went and cried in the toilet when my birthday came.

JACOB *seeing* RALPH *remove his tie:* You're going to bed?

RALPH: No, I'm putting on a clean shirt.

JACOB: Why?

RALPH: I got a girl. . . . Don't laugh!

JACOB: Who laughs? Since when?

RALPH: Three weeks. She lives in Yorkville with an aunt and uncle. A bunch of relatives, but no parents.

JACOB: An orphan girl—tch, tch.

RALPH: But she's got me! Boy, I'm telling you I could sing! Jake, she's like stars. She's so beautiful you look at her and cry! She's like French words! We went to the park the other night. Heard the last band concert.

JACOB: Music. . . .

RALPH *stuffing shirt in trousers:* It got cold and I gave her my coat to wear. We just walked along like that, see, without a word, see. I never was so happy in all my life. It got late . . . we just sat there. She looked at me—you know what I mean, how a girl looks at you—right in the eyes? "I love you," she says, "Ralph." I took her home. . . . I wanted to cry. That's how I felt!

JACOB: It's a beautiful feeling.

RALPH: You said a mouthful!

JACOB: Her name is——

RALPH: Blanche.

JACOB: A fine name. Bring her sometimes here.

RALPH: She's scared to meet Mom.

JACOB: Why?

RALPH: You know Mom's not letting my sixteen bucks out of the house if she can help it. She'd take one look at Blanche and insult her in a minute —a kid who's got nothing.

JACOB: Boychick!

RALPH: What's the diff?

JACOB: It's no difference—a plain bourgeois prejudice—but when they find out a poor girl—it ain't so kosher.

RALPH: They don't have to know I've got a girl.

JACOB: What's in the end?

RALPH: Out I go! I don't mean maybe!

JACOB: And then what?

RALPH: Life begins.

JACOB: What life?

RALPH: Life with my girl. Boy, I could sing when I think about it! Her and me together—that's a new life!

JACOB: Don't make a mistake! A new death!

RALPH: What's the idea?

JACOB: Me, I'm the idea! Once I had in *my* heart a dream, a vision, but came marriage and then you forget. Children come and you forget because——

RALPH: Don't worry, Jake.

JACOB: Remember, a woman insults a man's soul like no other thing in the whole world!

RALPH: Why get so excited? No one——

JACOB: Boychick, wake up! Be something! Make your life something good. For the love of an old man who sees in your young days his new life, for such love take the world in your two hands and make it like new. Go out and fight so life shouldn't be printed on dollar bills. A woman waits.

RALPH: Say, I'm no fool!

JACOB: From my heart I hope not. In the meantime——

Bell rings.

RALPH: See who it is, will you? *Stands off.* Don't want Mom to catch me with a clean shirt.

JACOB *calls:* Come in. *Sotto voce:* Moe Axelrod.

MOE *enters.*

MOE: Hello girls, how's your whiskers? *To* RALPH: All dolled up. What's it, the weekly visit to the cat house?

RALPH: Please mind your business.

MOE: Okay, sweetheart.

RALPH *taking a hidden dollar from a book:* If Mom asks where I went——

JACOB: I know. Enjoy yourself

RALPH: Bye-bye. *He exits.*

JACOB: Bye-bye.

MOE: Who's home?

JACOB: Me.

MOE: Good. I'll stick around a few minutes. Where's Hennie?

JACOB: She went with Bessie and Myron to a show.

MOE: She what?!

JACOB: You had a date?

MOE *hiding his feelings:* Here—I brought you some halavah.

JACOB: Halavah? Thanks. I'll eat a piece after.

MOE: So Ralph's got a dame? Hot stuff—a kid can't even play a card game.

JACOB: Moe, you're a no-good, a bum of the first water. To your dying day you won't change.

MOE: Where'd you get that stuff, a no-good?

JACOB: But I like you.

MOE: Didn't I go fight in France for democracy? Didn't I get my goddam leg shot off in that war the day before the armistice? Uncle Sam give

me the Order of the Purple Heart, didn't he?
What'd you mean, a no-good?

JACOB: Excuse me.

MOE: If you got an orange I'll eat an orange.

JACOB: No orange. An apple.

MOE: No oranges, huh?—what a dump!

JACOB: Bessie hears you once talking like this
she'll knock your head off.

MOE: Hennie went with, huh? She wantsa see
me squirm, only I don't squirm for dames.

JACOB: You came to see her?

MOE: What for? I got a present for our boy
friend, Myron. He'll drop dead when I tell him
his gentle horse galloped in fifteen to one. He'll die.

JACOB: It really won? The first time I remember.

MOE: Where'd they go?

JACOB: A vaudeville by the Franklin.

MOE: What's special tonight?

JACOB: Someone tells a few jokes...and they
forget the street is filled with starving beggars.

MOE: What'll they do—start a war?

JACOB: I don't know.

MOE: You oughta know. What the hell you got
all the books for?

JACOB: It needs a new world.

MOE: That's why they had the big war—to
make a new world, they said—safe for democracy.
Sure every big general laying up in a Paris hotel

with a half dozen broads pinned on his mustache. Democracy! I learned a lesson.

JACOB: An imperial war. You know what this means?

MOE: Sure, I know everything!

JACOB: By money men the interests must be protected. Who gave you such a rotten haircut? Please, *fishing in his vest pocket*, give me for a cent a cigarette. I didn't have since yesterday——

MOE *giving one*: Don't make me laugh. *A cent passes back and forth between them*, MOE *finally throwing it over his shoulder*. Don't look so tired all the time. You're a wow—always sore about something.

JACOB: And you?

MOE: You got one thing—you can play pinochle. I'll take you over in a game. Then you'll have something to be sore on.

JACOB: Who'll wash dishes?

MOE *takes deck from buffet drawer*.

MOE: Do 'em after. Ten cents a deal.

JACOB: Who's got ten cents?

MOE: I got ten cents. I'll lend it to you.

JACOB: Commence.

MOE *shaking cards*: The first time I had my hands on a pack in two days. Lemme shake up these cards. I'll make 'em talk.

JACOB *goes to his room where he puts on a Caruso record*.

JACOB: You should live so long.

MOE: Ever see oranges grow? I know a certain place——— One summer I laid under a tree and let them fall right in my mouth.

JACOB *off the music is playing; the card game begins:* From "L'Africana" ... a big explorer comes on a new land—"O Paradiso." From act four this piece. Caruso stands on the ship and looks on a Utopia. You hear? "Oh paradise! Oh paradise on earth! Oh blue sky, oh fragrant air———"

MOE: Ask him does he see any oranges?

BESSIE, MYRON *and* HENNIE *enter.*

JACOB: You came back so soon?

BESSIE: Hennie got sick on the way.

MYRON: Hello, Moe....

MOE *puts cards back in pocket.*

BESSIE: Take off the phonograph, Pop. *To* HENNIE: Lay down ... I'll call the doctor. You should see how she got sick on Prospect Avenue. Two weeks already she don't feel right.

MYRON: Moe ... ?

BESSIE: Go to bed, Hennie.

HENNIE: I'll sit here.

BESSIE: Such a girl I never saw! Now you'll be stubborn?

MYRON: It's for your own good, Beauty. Influenza———

HENNIE: I'll sit here.

BESSIE: You ever seen a girl should say no to everything. She can't stand on her feet, so———

HENNIE: Don't yell in my ears. I hear. Nothing's wrong. I ate tuna fish for lunch.

MYRON: Canned goods. . . .

BESSIE: Last week you also ate tuna fish?

HENNIE: Yeah, I'm funny for tuna fish. Go to the show—have a good time.

BESSIE: I don't understand what I did to God He blessed me with such children. From the whole world——

MOE *coming to aid of* HENNIE: For Chris' sake, don't kibitz so much!

BESSIE: You don't like it?

MOE *aping*: No, I don't like it.

BESSIE: That's too bad, Axelrod. Maybe it's better by your cigar store friends. Here we're different people.

MOE: Don't gimme that cigar store line, Bessie. I walked up five flights——

BESSIE: To take out Hennie. But my daughter ain't in your class, Axelrod.

MOE: To see Myron.

MYRON: Did he, did he, Moe?

MOE: Did he what?

MYRON: "Sky Rocket"?

BESSIE: You bet on a horse!

MOE: Paid twelve and a half to one.

MYRON: There! you hear that, Momma? Our horse came in. You see, it happens, and twelve and a half to one. Just look at that!

MOE: What the hell, a sure thing. I told you.

BESSIE: If Moe said a sure thing, you couldn't bet a few dollars instead of fifty cents?

JACOB *laughs:* "Aie, aie, aie."

MOE *at his wallet:* I'm carrying six hundred "plunks" in big denominations.

BESSIE: A banker!

MOE: Uncle Sam sends me ninety a month.

BESSIE: So you save it?

MOE: Run it up, Run-it-up-Axelrod, that's me.

BESSIE: The police should know how.

MOE *shutting her up:* All right, all right— Change twenty, sweetheart.

MYRON: Can you make change?

BESSIE: Don't be crazy.

MOE: I'll meet a guy in Goldman's restaurant. I'll meet 'im and come back with change.

MYRON *figuring on paper:* You can give it to me tomorrow in the store.

BESSIE *acquisitive:* He'll come back, he'll come back!

MOE: Lucky I bet some bucks myself. *In derision to* HENNIE: Let's step out tomorrow night, Par-a-dise. *Thumbs his nose at her, laughs mordantly and exits.*

MYRON: Oh, that's big percentage. If I picked a winner every day. . . .

BESSIE: Poppa, did you take Tootsie on the roof?

JACOB: All right.

MYRON: Just look at that—a cake walk. We can make——

BESSIE: It's enough talk. I got a splitting head-ache. Hennie, go in bed. I'll call Dr. Cantor.

HENNIE: I'll sit here . . . and don't call that old Ignatz 'cause I won't see him.

MYRON: If you get sick Momma can't nurse you. You don't want to go to a hospital.

JACOB: She don't look sick, Bessie, it's a fact.

BESSIE: She's got fever. I see in her eyes, so he tells me no. Myron, call Dr. Cantor.

MYRON *picks up phone, but* HENNIE *grabs it from him.*

HENNIE: I don't want any doctor. I ain't sick. Leave me alone.

MYRON: Beauty, it's for your own sake.

HENNIE: Day in and day out pestering. Why are you always right and no one else can say a word?

BESSIE: When you have your own children——

HENNIE: I'm not sick! Hear what I say? I'm not sick! Nothing's the matter with me! I don't want a doctor.

BESSIE *is watching her with slow progressive understanding.*

BESSIE: What's the matter?

HENNIE: Nothing, I told you!

BESSIE: You told me, but——

A long pause of examination follows.

HENNIE: See much?

BESSIE: Myron, put down the . . . the . . . . *He*

AWAKE AND SING!

slowly puts the phone down. Tell me what happened....

HENNIE: Brooklyn Bridge fell down.

BESSIE *approaching:* I'm asking a question....

MYRON: What's happened, Momma?

BESSIE: Listen to me!

HENNIE: What the hell are you talking?

BESSIE: Poppa—take Tootsie on the roof.

HENNIE *holding* JACOB *back:* If he wants he can stay here.

MYRON: What's wrong, Momma?

BESSIE *her voice quivering slightly:* Myron, your fine Beauty's in trouble. Our society lady....

MYRON: Trouble? I don't under—is it——?

BESSIE: Look in her face. *He looks, understands and slowly sits in a chair, utterly crushed.* Who's the man?

HENNIE: The Prince of Wales.

BESSIE: My gall is busting in me. In two seconds——

HENNIE *in a violent outburst:* Shut up! Shut up! I'll jump out the window in a minute! Shut up! *Finally she gains control of herself, says in a low, hard voice:* You don't know him.

JACOB: Bessie....

BESSIE: He's a Bronx boy?

HENNIE: From out of town.

BESSIE: What do you mean?

HENNIE: From out of town!!

BESSIE: A long time you know him? You were

41

sleeping by a girl from the office Saturday nights? You slept good, my lovely lady. You'll go to him ... he'll marry you.

HENNIE: That's what you say.

BESSIE: That's what I say! He'll do it, take MY word he'll do it!

HENNIE: Where? *To* JACOB: Give her the letter.

JACOB *does so.*

BESSIE: What? *Reads.* "Dear sir: In reply to your request of the 14th inst., we can state that no Mr. Ben Grossman has ever been connected with our organization..." You don't know where he is?

HENNIE: No.

BESSIE *walks back and forth:* Stop crying like a baby, Myron.

MYRON: It's like a play on the stage....

BESSIE: To a mother you couldn't say something before. I'm old-fashioned—like your friends I'm not smart—I don't eat chop suey and run around Coney Island with tramps. *She walks reflectively to buffet, picks up a box of candy, puts it down, says to Myron:* Tomorrow night bring Sam Feinschreiber for supper.

HENNIE: I won't do it.

BESSIE: You'll do it, my fine beauty, you'll do it!

HENNIE: I'm not marrying a poor foreigner like him. Can't even speak an English word. Not me! I'll go to my grave without a husband.

BESSIE: You don't say! We'll find for you somewhere a millionaire with a pleasure boat. He's going to night school, Sam. For a boy only three years in the country he speaks very nice. In three years he put enough in the bank, a good living.

JACOB: This is serious?

BESSIE: What then? I'm talking for my health? He'll come tomorrow night for supper. By Saturday they're engaged.

JACOB: Such a thing you can't do.

BESSIE: Who asked your advice?

JACOB: Such a thing——

BESSIE: Never mind!

JACOB: The lowest from the low!

BESSIE: Don't talk! I'm warning you! A man who don't believe in God—with crazy ideas——

JACOB: So bad I never imagined you could be.

BESSIE: Maybe if you didn't talk so much it wouldn't happen like this. You with your ideas— I'm a mother. I raise a family they should have respect!

JACOB: Respect? *Spits.* Respect! For the neighbors' opinion! You insult me, Bessie!

BESSIE: Go in your room, Papa. Every job he ever had he lost because he's got a big mouth. He opens his mouth and the whole Bronx could fall in. Everybody said it——

MYRON: Momma, they'll hear you down the dumbwaiter.

BESSIE: A good barber not to hold a job a week. Maybe you never heard charity starts at home. You never heard it, Pop?

JACOB: All you know, I heard, and more yet. But Ralph you don't make like you. Before you do it, I'll die first. He'll find a girl. He'll go in a fresh world with her. This is a house? Marx said it—abolish such families.

BESSIE: Go in your room, Papa.

JACOB: Ralph you don't make like you!

BESSIE: Go lay in your room with Caruso and the books together.

JACOB: All right!

BESSIE: Go in the room!

JACOB: Some day I'll come out I'll—— *Unable to continue, he turns, looks at* HENNIE, *goes to his door and there says with an attempt at humor:* Bessie, some day you'll talk to me so fresh...I'll leave the house for good! *He exits.*

BESSIE *crying:* You ever in your life seen it? He should dare! He should just dare say in the house another word. Your gall could bust from such a man. *Bell rings,* MYRON *goes.* Go to sleep now. It won't hurt.

HENNIE: Yeah?

MOE *enters, a box in his hand.* MYRON *follows and sits down.*

MOE *looks around first—putting box on table:* Cake. *About to give* MYRON *the money, he turns instead to* BESSIE: Six fifty, four bits change... come on, hand over half a buck. *She does so. Of* MYRON: Who bit him?

BESSIE: We're soon losing our Hennie, Moe.

MOE: Why? What's the matter?

BESSIE: She made her engagement.

MOE: Zat so?

BESSIE: Today it happened ... he asked her.

MOE: Did he? Who? Who's the corpse?

BESSIE: It's a secret.

MOE: In the bag, huh?

HENNIE: Yeah....

BESSIE: When a mother gives away an only daughter it's no joke. Wait, when you'll get married you'll know....

MOE *bitterly:* Don't make me laugh—when I get married! What I think a women? Take 'em all, cut 'em in little pieces like a herring in Greek salad. A guy in France had the right idea— dropped his wife in a bathtub fulla acid. *Whistles.* Sss, down the pipe! Pfft—not even a corset button left!

MYRON: Corsets don't have buttons.

MOE *to* HENNIE: What's the great idea? Gone big time, Paradise? Christ, it's suicide! Sure, kids you'll have, gold teeth, get fat, big in the tangerines——

HENNIE: Shut your face!

MOE: Who's it—some dope pullin' down twenty bucks a week? Cut your throat, sweetheart. Save time.

BESSIE: Never mind your two cents, Axelrod.

MOE: I say what I think—that's me!

HENNIE: That's you—a lousy four flusher who'd steal the glasses off a blind man.

MOE: Get hot!

HENNIE: My God, do I need it—to listen to this mutt shoot his mouth off?

MYRON: Please. . . .

MOE: Now wait a minute, sweetheart, wait a minute. I don't have to take that from you.

BESSIE: Don't yell at her!

HENNIE: For two cents I'd spit in your eye.

MOE *throwing coin to table:* Here's two bits.

HENNIE *looks at him and then starts across the room.*

BESSIE: Where are you going?

HENNIE *crying:* For my beauty nap, Mussolini. Wake me up when it's apple blossom time in Normandy. *Exits.*

MOE: Pretty, pretty—a sweet gal, your Hennie. See the look in her eyes?

BESSIE: She don't feel well. . . .

MYRON: Canned goods. . . .

BESSIE: So don't start with her.

MOE: Like a battleship she's got it. Not like other dames—shove 'em and they lay. Not her. I got a yen for her and I don't mean a Chinee coin.

BESSIE: Listen, Axelrod, in my house you don't talk this way. Either have respect or get out.

MOE: When I think about it . . . maybe I'd marry her myself.

46

BESSIE *suddenly aware of* MOE: You could——
What do you mean, Moe?

MOE: You ain't sunburnt—you heard me.

BESSIE: Why don't you, Moe? An old friend of
the family like you. It would be a blessing on all
of us.

MOE: You said she's engaged.

BESSIE: But maybe she don't know her own
mind. Say, it's——

MOE: I need a wife like a hole in the head. . . .
What's to know about women, I know. Even if I
asked her. She won't do it! A guy with one leg—
it gives her the heebie-jeebies. I know what she's
looking for. An arrow collar guy, a hero, but with
a wad of jack. Only the two don't go together. But
I got what it takes . . . plenty, and more where it
comes from. . . . *Breaks off, snorts and rubs his
knee. A pause. In his room* JACOB *puts on Caruso
singing the lament from "The Pearl Fishers."*

BESSIE: It's right—she wants a millionaire with
a mansion on Riverside Drive. So go fight City
Hall. Cake?

MOE: Cake.

BESSIE: I'll make tea. But one thing—she's got a
fine boy with a business brain. Caruso! *Exits into
the front room and stands in the dark, at the
window.*

MOE: No wet smack . . . a fine girl. . . . She'll
burn that guy out in a month. MOE *retrieves the
quarter and spins it on the table.*

47

MYRON: I remember that song ... beautiful. Nora Bayes sang it at the old Proctor's Twenty-third Street—"When It's Apple Blossom Time in Normandy." ...

MOE: She wantsa see me crawl—my head on a plate she wants! A snowball in hell's got a better chance. *Out of sheer fury he spins the quarter in his fingers.*

MYRON *as his eyes slowly fill with tears:* Beautiful ...

MOE: Match you for a quarter. Match you for any goddam thing you got. *Spins the coin viciously.* What the hell kind of house is this it ain't got an orange!!

SLOW CURTAIN

ACT · II

ACT · II

Scene I

One year later, a Sunday after-noon. The front room. JACOB *is giving his son* MORDECAI (UNCLE MORTY) *a haircut, newspapers spread around the base of the chair.* MOE *is reading a newspaper, leg propped on a chair.* RALPH, *in another chair, is spasmodically reading a paper.* UNCLE MORTY *reads colored jokes. Silence, then* BESSIE *enters.*

BESSIE: Dinner's in half an hour, Morty.

MORTY *still reading jokes:* I got time.

BESSIE: A duck. Don't get hair on the rug, Pop. *Goes to window and pulls down shade.* What's the matter the shade's up to the ceiling?

JACOB *pulling it up again:* Since when do I give a haircut in the dark? *He mimics her tone.*

BESSIE: When you're finished, pull it down. I like my house to look respectable. Ralphie, bring up two bottles seltzer from Weiss.

RALPH: I'm reading the paper.

BESSIE: Uncle Morty likes a little seltzer.

RALPH: I'm expecting a phone call.

BESSIE: Noo, if it comes you'll be back. What's

the matter? *Gives him money from apron pocket.*
Take down the old bottles.

RALPH *to* JACOB: Get that call if it comes. Say
I'll be right back.

JACOB *nods assent.*

MORTY *giving change from vest*: Get grandpa
some cigarettes.

RALPH: Okay. *Exits.*

JACOB: What's new in the paper, Moe?

MOE: Still jumping off the high buildings like
flies—the big shots who lost all their cocoanuts.
Pfft!

JACOB: Suicides?

MOE: Plenty can't take it—good in the break,
but can't take the whip in the stretch.

MORTY *without looking up*: I saw it happen
Monday in my building. My hair stood up how
they shoveled him together—like a pancake—a
bankrupt manufacturer.

MOE: No brains.

MORTY: Enough . . . all over the sidewalk.

JACOB: If someone said five-ten years ago I
couldn't make for myself a living, I wouldn't believe—

MORTY: Duck for dinner?

BESSIE: The best Long Island duck.

MORTY: I like goose.

BESSIE: A duck is just like a goose, only better.

MORTY: I like a goose.

BESSIE: The next time you'll be for Sunday dinner I'll make a goose.

MORTY *sniffs deeply:* Smells good. I'm a great boy for smells.

BESSIE: Ain't you ashamed? Once in a blue moon he should come to an only sister's house.

MORTY: Bessie, leave me live.

BESSIE: You should be ashamed!

MORTY: Quack quack!

BESSIE: No, better to lay around Mecca Temple playing cards with the Masons.

MORTY *with good nature:* Bessie, don't you see Pop's giving me a haircut?

BESSIE: You don't need no haircut. Look, two hairs he took off.

MORTY: Pop likes to give me a haircut. If I said no he don't forget for a year, do you, Pop? An old man's like that.

JACOB: I still do an A-1 job.

MORTY *winking:* Pop cuts hair to fit the face, don't you, Pop?

JACOB: For sure, Morty. To each face a different haircut. Custom built, no ready made. A round face needs special——

BESSIE *cutting him short:* A graduate from the B.M.T. *Going:* Don't forget the shade. *The phone rings. She beats* JACOB *to it.* Hello? Who is it, please? ... Who is it please? ... Miss Hirsch? No, he ain't here. ... No, I couldn't say when. *Hangs up sharply.*

JACOB: For Ralph?

BESSIE: A wrong number.

JACOB *looks at her and goes back to his job.*

JACOB: Excuse me!

BESSIE *to* MORTY: Ralphie took another cut down the place yesterday.

MORTY: Business is bad. I saw his boss Harry Glicksman Thursday. I bought some velvets... they're coming in again.

BESSIE: Do something for Ralphie down there.

MORTY: What can I do? I mentioned it to Glicksman. He told me they squeezed out half the people....

MYRON *enters dressed in apron.*

BESSIE: What's gonna be the end? Myron's working only three days a week now.

MYRON: It's conditions.

BESSIE: Hennie's married with a baby... money just don't come in. I never saw conditions should be so bad.

MORTY: Times'll change.

MOE: The only thing'll change is my underwear.

MORTY: These last few years I got my share of gray hairs. *Still reading jokes without having looked up once.* Ha, ha, ha—Pop Eye the sailor ate spinach and knocked out four bums.

MYRON: I'll tell you the way I see it. The country needs a great man now—a regular Teddy Roosevelt.

MOE: What this country needs is a good five-cent earthquake.

JACOB: So long labor lives it should increase private gain——

BESSIE *to* JACOB: Listen, Poppa, go talk on the street corner. The government'll give you free board the rest of your life.

MORTY: I'm surprised. Don't I send a five-dollar check for Pop every week?

BESSIE: You could afford a couple more and not miss it.

MORTY: Tell me jokes. Business is so rotten I could just as soon lay all day in the turkish bath.

MYRON: Why'd I come in here? *Puzzled, he exits.*

MORTY *to* MOE: I hear the bootleggers still do business, Moe.

MOE: Wake up! I kissed bootlegging bye-bye two years back.

MORTY: For a fact? What kind of racket is it now?

MOE: If I told you, you'd know something.

HENNIE *comes from bedroom.*

HENNIE: Where's Sam?

BESSIE: Sam? In the kitchen.

HENNIE *calls:* Sam. Come take the diaper.

MORTY: How's the Mickey Louse? Ha, ha, ha. . . .

HENNIE: Sleeping.

MORTY: Ah, that's life to a baby. He sleeps—

gets it in the mouth—sleeps some more. To raise a family nowadays you must be a damn fool.

BESSIE: Never mind, never mind, a woman who don't raise a family—a girl—should jump overboard. What's she good for? *To* MOE—*to change the subject:* Your leg bothers you bad?

MOE: It's okay, sweetheart.

BESSIE *to* MORTY: It hurts him every time it's cold out. He's got four legs in the closet.

MORTY: Four wooden legs?

MOE: Three.

MORTY: What's the big idea?

MOE: Why not? Uncle Sam gives them out free.

MORTY: Say, maybe if Uncle Sam gave out less legs we could balance the budget.

JACOB: Or not have a war so they wouldn't have to give out legs.

MORTY: Shame on you, Pop. Everybody knows war is necessary.

MOE: Don't make me laugh. Ask me—the first time you pick up a dead one in the trench—then you learn war ain't so damn necessary.

MORTY: Say, you should kick. The rest of your life Uncle Sam pays you ninety a month. Look, not a worry in the world.

MOE: Don't make me laugh. Uncle Sam can take his *seventy* bucks and—— *Finishes with a gesture.* Nothing good hurts! *He rubs his stump.*

HENNIE: Use a crutch, Axelrod. Give the stump a rest.

MOE: Mind your business, Feinschreiber.

BESSIE: It's a sensible idea.

MOE: Who asked you?

BESSIE: Look, he's ashamed.

MOE: So's your Aunt Fanny.

BESSIE *naïvely*: Who's got an Aunt Fanny? *She cleans a rubber plant's leaves with her apron.*

MORTY: It's a joke!

MOE: I don't want my paper creased before I read it. I want it fresh. Fifty times I said that.

BESSIE: Don't get so excited for a five-cent paper—our star boarder.

MOE: And I don't want no one using my razor either. Get it straight. I'm not buying ten blades a week for the Berger family. *Furious, he limps out.*

BESSIE: Maybe I'm using his razor too.

HENNIE: Proud!

BESSIE: You need luck with plants. I didn't clean off the leaves in a month.

MORTY: You keep the house like a pin and I like your cooking. Any time Myron fires you, come to me, Bessie. I'll let the butler go and you'll be my housekeeper. I don't like Japs so much—sneaky.

BESSIE: Say you can't tell. Maybe any day I'm coming to stay.

HENNIE *exits.*

JACOB: Finished.

MORTY: How much, Ed. Pinaud? *Disengages self from chair.*

JACOB: Five cents.

MORTY: Still five cents for a haircut to fit the face?

JACOB: Prices don't change by me. *Takes a dollar.* I can't change——

MORTY: Keep it. Buy yourself a Packard. Ha, ha, ha.

JACOB *taking large envelope from pocket:* Please, you'll keep this for me. Put it away.

MORTY: What is it?

JACOB: My insurance policy. I don't like it should lay around where something could happen.

MORTY: What could happen?

JACOB: Who knows, robbers, fire . . . they took next door. Fifty dollars from O'Reilly.

MORTY: Say, lucky a Berger didn't lose it.

JACOB: Put it downtown in the safe. Bessie don't have to know.

MORTY: It's made out to Bessie?

JACOB: No, to Ralph.

MORTY: To Ralph?

JACOB: He don't know. Someday he'll get three thousand.

MORTY: You got good years ahead.

JACOB: Behind.

RALPH *enters.*

RALPH: Cigarettes. Did a call come?

JACOB: A few minutes. She don't let me answer it.

RALPH: Did Mom say I was coming back?

JACOB: No.

MORTY *is back at new jokes.*

RALPH: She starting that stuff again? BESSIE *enters.* A call come for me?

BESSIE *waters pot from milk bottle:* A wrong number.

JACOB: Don't say a lie, Bessie.

RALPH: Blanche said she'd call me at two—was it her?

BESSIE: I said a wrong number.

RALPH: Please Mom, if it was her tell me.

BESSIE: YOU call me a liar next. You got no shame—to start a scene in front of Uncle Morty. Once in a blue moon he comes——

RALPH: What's the shame? If my girl calls I wanna know it.

BESSIE: You made enough mish mosh with her until now.

MORTY: I'm surprised, Bessie. For the love of Mike tell him yes or no.

BESSIE: I didn't tell him? No!

MORTY *to* RALPH: No!

RALPH *goes to a window and looks out.*

BESSIE: Morty, I didn't say before—he runs around steady with a girl.

MORTY: Terrible. Should he run around with a foxie-woxie?

59

BESSIE: A girl with no parents.

MORTY: An orphan?

BESSIE: I could die from shame. A year already he runs around with her. He brought her once for supper. Believe me, she didn't come again, no!

RALPH: Don't think I didn't ask her.

BESSIE: You hear? You raise them and what's in the end for all your trouble?

JACOB: When you'll lay in a grave, no more trouble. *Exits.*

MORTY: Quack quack!

BESSIE: A girl like that he wants to marry. A skinny consumptive-looking ... six months already she's not working—taking charity from an aunt. You should see her. In a year she's dead on his hands.

RALPH: You'd cut her throat if you could.

BESSIE: That's right! Before she'd ruin a nice boy's life I would first go to prison. Miss Nobody should step in the picture and I'll stand by with my mouth shut.

RALPH: Miss Nobody! Who am I? Al Jolson?

BESSIE: Fix your tie!

RALPH: I'll take care of my own life.

BESSIE: You'll take care? Excuse my expression, you can't even wipe your nose yet! He'll take care!

MORTY *to* BESSIE: I'm surprised. Don't worry so much, Bessie. When it's time to settle down he won't marry a poor girl, will you? In the long run common sense is thicker than love. I'm a great boy for live and let live.

BESSIE: Sure, it's easy to say. In the meantime he eats out my heart. You know I'm not strong.

MORTY: I know . . . a pussy cat . . . ha, ha, ha.

BESSIE: You got money and money talks. But without the dollar who sleeps at night?

RALPH: I been working for years, bringing in money here—putting it in your hand like a kid. All right, I can't get my teeth fixed. All right, that a new suit's like trying to buy the Chrysler Building. You never in your life bought me a pair of skates even—things I died for when I was a kid. I don't care about that stuff, see. Only just remember I pay some of the bills around here, just a few . . . and if my girl calls me on the phone I'll talk to her any time I please. *He exits.* HENNIE *applauds.*

BESSIE: Don't be so smart! Miss America! *To* MORTY: He didn't have skates! But when he got sick, a twelve-year-old boy, who called a big specialist for the last $25 in the house? Skates!

JACOB *just in. Adjusts window shade:* It looks like snow today.

MORTY: It's about time—winter.

BESSIE: Poppa here could talk like Samuel Webster, too, but it's just talk. He should try to buy a two-cent pickle in the Burland Market without money.

MORTY: I'm getting an appetite.

BESSIE: Right away we'll eat. I made chopped liver for you.

MORTY: My specialty!

BESSIE: Ralph should only be a success like you, Morty. I should only live to see the day when he rides up to the door in a big car with a chauffeur and a radio. I could die happy, believe me.

MORTY: Success she says. She should see how we spend thousands of dollars making up a winter line and winter don't come—summer in January. Can you beat it?

JACOB: Don't live, just make success.

MORTY: Chopped liver—ha!

JACOB: Ha! *Exits.*

MORTY: When they start arguing, I don't hear. Suddenly I'm deaf. I'm a great boy for the practical side. *He looks over to* HENNIE *who sits rubbing hands with lotion.*

HENNIE: Hands like a raw potato.

MORTY: What's the matter? You don't look so well . . . no pep.

HENNIE: I'm swell.

MORTY: You used to be such a pretty girl.

HENNIE: Maybe I got the blues. You can't tell.

MORTY: You could stand a new dress.

HENNIE: That's not all I could stand.

MORTY: Come down to the place tomorrow and pick out a couple from the "eleven-eighty" line. Only don't sing me the blues.

HENNIE: Thanks. I need some new clothes.

MORTY: I got two thousand pieces of merchandise waiting in the stock room for winter.

HENNIE: I never had anything from life. Sam don't help.

MORTY: He's crazy about the kid.

HENNIE: Crazy is right. Twenty-one a week he brings in—a nigger don't have it so hard. I wore my fingers off on an Underwood for six years. For what? Now I wash baby diapers. Sure, I'm crazy about the kid too. But half the night the kid's up. Try to sleep. You don't know how it is, Uncle Morty.

MORTY: No, I don't know. I was born yesterday. Ha, ha, ha. Some day I'll leave you a little nest egg. You like eggs? Ha?

HENNIE: When? When I'm dead and buried?

MORTY: No, when *I'm* dead and buried. Ha, ha, ha.

HENNIE: You should know what I'm thinking.

MORTY: Ha, ha, ha, I know.

MYRON *enters.*

MYRON: I never take a drink. I'm just surprised at myself, I——

MORTY: I got a pain. Maybe I'm hungry.

MYRON: Come inside, Morty. Bessie's got some schnapps.

MORTY: I'll take a drink. Yesterday I missed the Turkish bath.

MYRON: I get so bitter when I take a drink, it just surprises me.

63

MORTY: Look how fat. Say, you live once.... Quack, quack. *Both exit.*

MOE *stands silently in the doorway.*

SAM *entering:* I'll make Leon's bottle now!

HENNIE: No, let him sleep, Sam. Take away the diaper. *He does. Exits.*

MOE *advancing into the room:* That your husband?

HENNIE: Don't you know?

MOE: Maybe he's a nurse you hired for the kid—it looks it—how he tends it. A guy comes howling to your old lady every time you look cock-eyed. Does he sleep with you?

HENNIE: Don't be so wise!

MOE *indicating newspaper:* Here's a dame strangled her hubby with wire. Claimed she didn't like him. Why don't you brain Sam with an ax some night?

HENNIE: Why don't you lay an egg, Axelrod?

MOE: I laid a few in my day, Feinschreiber. Hard-boiled ones too.

HENNIE: Yeah?

MOE: Yeah. You wanna know what I see when I look in your eyes?

HENNIE: No.

MOE: Ted Lewis playing the clarinet—some of those high crazy notes! Christ, you coulda had a guy with some guts instead of a cluck stands around boilin' baby nipples.

HENNIE: Meaning you?

64

MOE: Meaning me, sweetheart.

HENNIE: Think you're pretty good.

MOE: You'd know if I slept with you again.

HENNIE: I'll smack your face in a minute.

MOE: You do and I'll break your arm. *Holds up paper.* Take a look. *Reads:* "Ten-day luxury cruise to Havana." That's the stuff you coulda had. Put up at ritzy hotels, frenchie soap, champagne. Now you're tied down to "Snake-Eye" here. What for? What's it get you?...a 2 x 4 flat on 108th Street...a pain in the bustle it gets you.

HENNIE: What's it to you?

MOE: I know you from the old days. How you like to spend it! What I mean! Lizard skin shoes, perfume behind the ears.... You're in a mess, Paradise! Paradise—that's a hot one—yah, crazy to eat a knish at your own wedding.

HENNIE: I get it—you're jealous. You can't get me.

MOE: Don't make me laugh.

HENNIE: Kid Jailbird's been trying to make me for years. You'd give your other leg. I'm hooked? Maybe, but you're in the same boat. Only it's worse for you. I don't give a damn no more, but you gotta yen makes you——

MOE: Don't make me laugh.

HENNIE: Compared to you I'm sittin' on top of the world.

MOE: You're losing your looks. A dame don't stay young forever.

HENNIE: You're a liar. I'm only twenty-four.

MOE: When you comin' home to stay?

HENNIE: Wouldn't you like to know?

MOE: I'll get you again.

HENNIE: Think so?

MOE: Sure, whatever goes up comes down. You're easy—you remember—two for a nickel—a pushover! *Suddenly she slaps him. They both seem stunned.* What's the idea?

HENNIE: Go on ... break my arm.

MOE *as if saying "I love you"*: Listen, lousy.

HENNIE: Go on, do something!

MOE: Listen——

HENNIE: You're so damn tough!

MOE: You like me. *He takes her.*

HENNIE: Take your hand off! *Pushes him away.* Come around when it's a flood again and they put you in the ark with the animals. Not even then— if you was the last man!

MOE: Baby, if you had a dog I'd love the dog.

HENNIE: Gorilla! *Exits.*

RALPH *enters.*

RALPH: Were you here before?

MOE *sits*: What?

RALPH: When the call came for me?

MOE: What?

RALPH: The call came.

JACOB *enters.*

MOE *rubbing his leg*: No.

JACOB: Don't worry, Ralphie, she'll call back.

66

RALPH: Maybe not. I think something's the matter.

JACOB: What?

RALPH: I don't know. I took her home from the movie last night. She asked me what I'd think if she went away.

JACOB: Don't worry, she'll call again.

RALPH: Maybe not, if Mom insulted her. She gets it on both ends, the poor kid. Lived in an orphan asylum most of her life. They shove her around like an empty freight train.

JACOB: After dinner go see her.

RALPH: Twice they kicked me down the stairs.

JACOB: Life should have some dignity.

RALPH: Every time I go near the place I get heart failure. The uncle drives a bus. You oughta see him—like Babe Ruth.

MOE: Use your brains. Stop acting like a kid who still wets the bed. Hire a room somewhere—a club room for two members.

RALPH: Not that kind of proposition, Moe.

MOE: Don't be a bush leaguer all your life.

RALPH: Cut it out!

MOE *on a sudden upsurge of emotion*: Ever sleep with one? Look at 'im blush.

RALPH: You don't know her.

MOE: I seen her—the kind no one sees undressed till the undertaker works on her.

RALPH: Why give me the needles all the time? What'd I ever do to you?

MOE: Not a thing. You're a nice kid. But grow up! In life there's two kinds—the men that's sure of themselves and the one's who ain't! It's time you quit being a selling-plater and got in the first class.

JACOB: And you, Axelrod?

MOE *to* JACOB: Scratch your whiskers! *To* RALPH: Get independent. Get what-it-takes and be yourself. Do what you like.

RALPH: Got a suggestion?

MORTY *enters, eating.*

MOE: Sure, pick out a racket. Shake down the cocoanuts. See what that does.

MORTY: We know what it does—puts a pudding on your nose! Sing, Sing! Easy money's against the law. Against the law don't win. A racket is illegitimate, no?

MOE: It's all a racket—from horse racing down. Marriage, politics, big business—everybody plays cops and robbers. You, you're a racketeer yourself.

MORTY: Who? Me? Personally I manufacture dresses.

MOE: Horse feathers!

MORTY *seriously:* Don't make such remarks to me without proof. I'm a great one for proof. That's why I made a success in business. Proof—put up or shut up, like a game of cards. I heard this remark before—a rich man's a crook who steals from the poor. Personally, I don't like it. It's a big lie!

MOE: If you don't like it, buy yourself a fife and drum—and go fight your own war.

MORTY: Sweatshop talk. Every Jew and Wop in the shop eats my bread and behind my back says, "a sonofabitch." I started from a poor boy who worked on an ice wagon for two dollars a week. Pop's right here—he'll tell you. I made it honest. In the whole industry nobody's got a better name.

JACOB: It's an exception, such success.

MORTY: Ralph can't do the same thing?

JACOB: No, Morty, I don't think. In a house like this he don't realize even the possibilities of life. Economics comes down like a ton of coal on the head.

MOE: Red rover, red rover, let Jacob come over!

JACOB: In my day the propaganda was for God. Now it's for success. A boy don't turn around without having shoved in him he should make success.

MORTY: Pop, you're a comedian, a regular Charlie Chaplin.

JACOB: He dreams all night of fortunes. Why not? Don't it say in the movies he should have a personal steamshop, pyjamas for fifty dollars a pair and a toilet like a monument? But in the morning he wakes up and for ten dollars he can't fix the teeth. And millions more worse off in the mills of the South—starvation wages. The blood from the worker's heart. MORTY *laughs loud and long.* Laugh, laugh ... tomorrow not.

MORTY: A real, a real Boob McNutt you're getting to be.

JACOB: Laugh, my son. . . .

MORTY: Here is the North, Pop.

JACOB: North, south, it's one country.

MORTY: The country's all right. A duck quacks in every pot!

JACOB: You never heard how they shoot down men and women which ask a better wage? Kentucky 1932?

MORTY: That's a pile of chopped liver, Pop.

BESSIE *and others enter.*

JACOB: Pittsburgh, Passaic, Illinois—slavery—it begins where success begins in a competitive system.

MORTY *howls with delight.*

MORTY: Oh Pop, what are you bothering? Why? Tell me why? Ha ha ha. I bought you a phonograph . . . stick to Caruso.

BESSIE: He's starting up again.

MORTY: Don't bother with Kentucky. It's full of moonshiners.

JACOB: Sure, sure——

MORTY: You don't know practical affairs. Stay home and cut hair to fit the face.

JACOB: It says in the Bible how the Red Sea opened and the Egyptians went in and the sea rolled over them. *Quotes two lines of Hebrew.* In this boy's life a Red Sea will happen again. I see it!

70

MORTY: I'm getting sore, Pop, with all this sweatshop talk.

BESSIE: He don't stop a minute. The whole day, like a phonograph.

MORTY: I'm surprised. Without a rich man you don't have a roof over your head. You don't know it?

MYRON: Now you can't bite the hand that feeds you.

RALPH: Let him alone—he's right!

BESSIE: Another county heard from.

RALPH: It's the truth. It's——

MORTY: Keep quiet, snotnose!

JACOB: For sure, charity, a bone for an old dog. But in Russia an old man don't take charity so his eyes turn black in his head. In Russia they got Marx.

MORTY *scoffingly:* Who's Marx?

MOE: An outfielder for the Yanks.

MORTY *howls with delight.*

MORTY: Ha ha ha, it's better than the jokes. I'm telling you. This is Uncle Sam's country. Put it in your pipe and smoke it.

BESSIE: Russia, he says! Read the papers.

SAM: Here is opportunity.

MYRON: People can't believe in God in Russia. The papers tell the truth, they do.

JACOB: So you believe in God . . . you got something for it? You! You worked for all the capitalists. You harvested the fruit from your labor? You

71

got God! But the past comforts you? The present smiles on you, yes? It promises you the future something? Did you found a piece of earth where you could live like a human being and die with the sun on your face? Tell me, yes, tell me. I would like to know myself. But on these questions, on this theme—the struggle for existence—you can't make an answer. The answer I see in your face ... the answer is your mouth can't talk. In this dark corner you sit and you die. But abolish private property!

BESSIE *settling the issue:* Noo, go fight City Hall!

MORTY: He's drunk!

JACOB: I'm studying from books a whole life-time.

MORTY: That's what it is—he's drunk. What the hell does all that mean?

JACOB: If you don't know, why should I tell you.

MORTY *triumphant at last:* You see? Hear him? Like all those nuts, don't know what they're saying.

JACOB: I know, I know.

MORTY: Like Boob McNutt you know! Don't go in the park, Pop—the squirrels'll get you. Ha, ha, ha....

BESSIE: Save your appetite, Morty. *To* MYRON: Don't drop the duck.

MYRON: We're ready to eat, Momma.

MORTY *to* JACOB: Shame on you. It's your second childhood.

Now they file out. MYRON *first with the duck, the others behind him.*

BESSIE: Come eat. We had enough for one day. *Exits.*

MORTY: Ha, ha, ha. Quack-quack. *Exits.*

JACOB *sits there trembling and deeply humiliated.* MOE *approaches him and thumbs the old man's nose in the direction of the dining room.*

MOE: Give 'em five. *Takes his hand away.* They got you pasted on the wall like a picture, Jake. *He limps out to seat himself at the table in the next room.*

JACOB: Go eat, boychick. RALPH *comes to him.* He gives me eat, so I'll climb in a needle. One time I saw an old horse in summer . . . he wore a straw hat . . . the ears stuck out on top. An old horse for hire. Give me back my young days . . . give me fresh blood . . . arms . . . give me—— *The telephone rings. Quickly* RALPH *goes to it.* JACOB *pulls the curtains and stands there, a sentry on guard.*

RALPH: Hello? . . . Yeah, I went to the store and came right back, right after you called. *Looks at Jacob.*

JACOB: Speak, speak. Don't be afraid they'll hear.

RALPH: I'm sorry if Mom said something. You know how excitable Mom is . . . Sure! What? . . .

Sure, I'm listening.... Put on the radio, Jake.
JACOB *does so. Music comes in and up, a tango,
grating with an insistent nostalgic pulse. Under
the cover of the music* RALPH *speaks more freely.*
Yes... yes... What's the matter? Why're you
crying? What happened? *To* JACOB: She's putting
her uncle on. Yes?... Listen, Mr. Hirsch, what're
you trying to do? What's the big idea? Honest to
God. I'm in no mood for joking! Lemme talk to
her! Gimme Blanche! *Waits.* Blanche? What's this?
Is this a joke? Is that true? I'm coming right
down! I know, but—— You wanna do that?... I
know, but—— I'm coming down... tonight!
Nine o'clock ... sure ... sure ... sure.... *Hangs
up.*

JACOB: What happened?

MORTY *enters:* Listen, Pop. I'm surprised you
didn't—— *He howls, shakes his head in mock de-
spair, exits.*

JACOB: Boychick, what?

RALPH: I don't get it straight. *To* JACOB: She's
leaving....

JACOB: Where?

RALPH: Out West—— To Cleveland.

JACOB: Cleveland?

RALPH: ... In a week or two. Can you picture
it? It's a put-up job. But they can't get away with
that.

JACOB: We'll find something.

74

RALPH: Sure, the angels of heaven'll come down on her uncle's cab and whisper in his ear.

JACOB: Come eat. . . . We'll find something.

RALPH: I'm meeting her tonight, but I know——

BESSIE *throws open the curtain between the two rooms and enters.*

BESSIE: Maybe we'll serve for you a special blue plate supper in the garden?

JACOB: All right, all right.

BESSIE *goes over to the window, levels the shade and on her way out, clicks off the radio.*

MORTY *within:* Leave the music, Bessie. *She clicks it on again, looks at them, exits.*

RALPH: I know . . .

JACOB: Don't cry, Boychick. *Goes over to Ralph.* Why should you make like this? Tell me why you should cry, just tell me. . . . JACOB *takes* RALPH *in his arms and both, trying to keep back the tears, trying fearfully not to be heard by the others in the dining room, begin crying.* You mustn't cry. . . .

The tango twists on. Inside the clatter of dishes and the clash of cutlery sound. MORTY *begins to howl with laughter.*

CURTAIN

ACT · II

Scene II
That night. The dark dining room.

At Rise
JACOB *is heard in his lighted room, reading from a sheet, declaiming aloud as if to an audience.*

JACOB: "They are there to remind us of the horrors—under those crosses lie hundreds of thousands of workers and farmers who murdered each other in uniform for the greater glory of capitalism. *Comes out of his room.* The new imperialist war will send millions to their death, will bring prosperity to the pockets of the capitalists—aie, Morty—and will bring only greater hunger and misery to the masses of workers and farmers. The memories of the last world slaughter are still vivid in our minds. *Hearing a noise he quickly retreats to his room.* RALPH *comes in from the street. He sits with hat and coat on.* JACOB *tentatively opens door and asks:* Ralphie?

RALPH: It's getting pretty cold out.

JACOB *enters room fully, cleaning hair clippers:* We should have steam till twelve instead of ten. Go complain to the Board of Health.

RALPH: It might snow,

76

JACOB: It don't hurt . . . extra work for men.

RALPH: When I was a kid I laid awake at nights and heard the sounds of trains . . . far-away lonesome sounds . . . boats going up and down the river. I used to think of all kinds of things I wanted to do. What was it, Jake? Just a bunch of noise in my head?

JACOB *waiting for news of the girl:* You wanted to make for yourself a certain kind of world.

RALPH: I guess I didn't. I'm feeling pretty, pretty low.

JACOB: You're a young boy and for you life is all in front like a big mountain. You got feet to climb.

RALPH: I don't know how.

JACOB: So you'll find out. Never a young man had such opportunity like today. He could make history.

RALPH: Ten P.M. and all is well. Where's everybody.

JACOB: They went.

RALPH: Uncle Morty too?

JACOB: Hennie and Sam he drove down.

RALPH: I saw her.

JACOB *alert and eager:* Yes, yes, tell me.

RALPH: I waited in Mount Morris Park till she came out. So cold I did a buck'n wing to keep warm. She's scared to death.

JACOB: They made her?

RALPH: Sure. She wants to go. They keep yell-

77

ing at her—they want her to marry a millionaire, too.

JACOB: You told her you love her?

RALPH: Sure. "Marry me," I said. "Marry me tomorrow." On sixteen bucks a week. On top of that I had to admit Mom'd have Uncle Morty get me fired in a second.... Two can starve as cheap as one!

JACOB: So what happened?

RALPH: I made her promise to meet me tomorrow.

JACOB: Now she'll go in the West?

RALPH: I'd fight the whole goddam world with her, but not her. No guts. The hell with her. If she wantsa go—all right—I'll get along.

JACOB: For sure, there's more important things than girls....

RALPH: You said a mouthful...and maybe I don't see it. She'll see what I can do. No one stops me when I get going.... *Near to tears, he has to stop.* JACOB *examines his clippers very closely.*

JACOB: Electric clippers never do a job like by hand.

RALPH: Why don't Mom let us live here?

JACOB: Why? Why? Because in a society like this today people don't love. Hate!

RALPH: Gee, I'm no bum who hangs around pool parlors. I got the stuff to go ahead. I don't know what to do.

JACOB: Look on me and learn what to do, boychick. Here sits an old man polishing tools. You think maybe I'll use them again! Look on this failure and see for seventy years he talked, with good ideas, but only in the head. It's enough for me now I should see your happiness. This is why I tell you— DO! Do what is in your heart and you carry in yourself a revolution. But you should act. Not like me. A man who had golden opportunities but drank instead a glass tea. No.... *A pause of silence.*

RALPH *listening:* Hear it? The Boston air mail plane. Ten minutes late. I get a kick the way it cuts across the Bronx every night. *The bell rings:*

SAM, *excited, disheveled, enters.*

JACOB: You came back so soon?

SAM: Where's Mom?

JACOB: Mom? Look on the chandelier.

SAM: Nobody's home?

JACOB: Sit down. Right away they're coming. You went in the street without a tie?

SAM: Maybe it's a crime.

JACOB: Excuse me.

RALPH: You had a fight with Hennie again?

SAM: She'll fight once... some day.... *Lapses into silence.*

JACOB: In my day the daughter came home. Now comes the son-in-law.

SAM: Once too often she'll fight with me, Hennie. I mean it. I mean it like anything. I'm a person with a bad heart. I sit quiet, but inside I got a——

RALPH: What happened?

SAM: I'll talk to Mom. I'll see Mom.

JACOB: Take an apple.

SAM: Please . . . he tells me apples.

RALPH: Why hop around like a billiard ball?

SAM: Even in a joke she should dare say it.

JACOB: My grandchild said something?

SAM: To my father in the old country they did a joke . . . I'll tell you: One day in Odessa he talked to another Jew on the street. They didn't like it, they jumped on him like a wild wolf.

RALPH: Who?

SAM: Cossacks. They cut off his beard. A Jew without a beard! He came home—I remember like yesterday how he came home and went in bed for two days. He put like this the cover on his face. No one should see. The third morning he died.

RALPH: From what?

SAM: From a broken heart. . . . Some people are like this. Me too. I could die like this from shame.

JACOB: Hennie told you something?

SAM: Straight out she said it—like a lightning from the sky. The baby ain't mine. She said it.

RALPH: Don't be a dope!

JACOB: For sure, a joke.

RALPH: She's kidding you.

SAM: She should kid a policeman, not Sam Fein-schreiber. Please . . . you don't know her like me. I wake up in the nighttime and she sits watching me like I don't know what. I make a nice living from the store. But it's no use—she looks for a star in the sky. I'm afraid like anything. You could go crazy from less even. What I shall do I'll ask Mom.

JACOB: "Go home and sleep," she'll say. "It's a bad dream."

SAM: It don't satisfy me more, such remarks, when Hennie could kill in the bed. JACOB *laughs.* Don't laugh. I'm so nervous—look, two times I weighed myself on the subway station. *Throws small cards to table.*

JACOB *examining one:* One hundred and thirty-eight—also a fortune. *Turns it and reads:* "You are inclined to deep thinking, and have a high admiration for intellectual excellence and inclined to be very exclusive in the selection of friends." Correct! I think maybe you got mixed up in the wrong family, Sam.

MYRON *and* BESSIE *now enter.*

BESSIE: Look, a guest! What's the matter? Something wrong with the baby? *Waits.*

SAM: No.

BESSIE: Noo?

SAM *in a burst:* I wash my hands from everything.

BESSIE: Take off your coat and hat. Have a seat. Excitement don't help. Myron, make tea. You'll have a glass tea. We'll talk like civilized people.

Myron goes. **W**hat is it, Ralph, you're all dressed up for a party? *He looks at her silently and exits.* *To* SAM: We saw a very good movie, with Wallace Beery. He acts like life, very good.

MYRON *within*: Polly Moran too.

BESSIE: Polly Moran too—a woman with a nose from here to Hunts Point, but a fine player. Poppa, take away the tools and the books.

JACOB: All right. *Exits to his room.*

BESSIE: Noo, Sam, why do you look like a funeral?

SAM: I can't stand it. . . .

BESSIES Wait. *Yells:* You took up Tootsie on the roof.

JACOB *within*: In a minute.

BESSIE: What can't you stand?

SAM: She said I'm a second fiddle in my own house.

BESSIE: Who?

SAM: Hennie. In the second place, it ain't my baby, she said.

BESSIE: What? What are you talking?

MYRON *enters with dishes.*

SAM: From her own mouth. It went like a knife in my heart.

BESSIE: Sam, what're you saying?

SAM: Please, I'm making a story? I fell in the chair like a dead.

BESSIE: Such a story you believe?

SAM: I don't know.

BESSIE: How you don't know?

SAM: She told me even the man.

BESSIE: Impossible!

SAM: I can't believe myself. But she said it. I'm a second fiddle, she said. She made such a yell everybody heard for ten miles.

BESSIE: Such a thing Hennie should say—impossible!

SAM: What should I do? With my bad heart such a remark kills.

MYRON: Hennie don't feel well, Sam. You see, she——

BESSIE: What then?—a sick girl. Believe me, a mother knows. Nerves. Our Hennie's got a bad temper. You'll let her she says anything. She takes after me—nervous. *To* MYRON: You ever heard such a remark in all your life? She should make such a statement! Bughouse.

MYRON: The little one's been sick all these months. Hennie needs a rest. No doubt.

BESSIE: Sam don't think she means it——

MYRON: Oh, I know he don't, of course——

BESSIE: I'll say the truth, Sam. We didn't half the time understand her ourselves. A girl with her own mind. When she makes it up, wild horses wouldn't change her.

SAM: She don't love me.

BESSIE: This is sensible, Sam?

SAM: Not for a nickel.

BESSIE: What do you think? She married you

for your money? For your looks? You ain't no John Barrymore, Sam. No, she liked you.

SAM: Please, not for a nickel.

JACOB *stands in the doorway.*

BESSIE: We stood right here the first time she said it. "Sam Feinschreiber's a nice boy," she said it, "a boy he's got good common sense, with a business head." Right here she said it, in this room. You sent her two boxes of candy together, you remember?

MYRON: Loft's candy.

BESSIE: This is when she said it. What do you think?

MYRON: You were just the only boy she cared for.

BESSIE: So she married you. Such a world... plenty of boy friends she had, believe me!

JACOB: A popular girl....

MYRON: Y-e-s.

BESSIE: I'll say it plain out—Moe Axelrod offered her plenty—a servant, a house... she don't have to pick up a hand.

MYRON: Oh, Moe? Just wild about her....

SAM: Moe Axelrod? He wanted to——

BESSIE: But she didn't care. A girl like Hennie you don't buy. I should never live to see another day if I'm telling a lie.

SAM: She was kidding me.

BESSIE: What then? You shouldn't be foolish.

SAM: The baby looks like my family. He's got Feinschreiber eyes.

BESSIE: A blind man could see it.

JACOB: Sure ... sure. ...

SAM: The baby looks like me. Yess. ...

BESSIE: You could believe me.

JACOB: Any day. ...

SAM: But she tells me the man. She made up his name too?

BESSIE: Sam, Sam, look in the phone book—a million names.

MYRON: Tom, Dick and Harry. JACOB *laughs quietly, soberly.*

BESSIE: Don't stand around, Poppa. Take Tootsie on the roof. And you don't let her go under the water tank.

JACOB: Schmah Yisroeal. Behold! *Quietly laughing he goes back into his room, closing the door behind him.*

SAM: I won't stand he should make insults. A man eats out his——

BESSIE: No, no, he's an old man—a second childhood. Myron, bring in the tea. Open a jar of raspberry jelly. MYRON *exits.*

SAM: Mom, you think——?

BESSIE: I'll talk to Hennie. It's all right.

SAM: Tomorrow, I'll take her by the doctor.

RALPH *enters.*

BESSIE: Stay for a little tea.

SAM: No, I'll go home. I'm tired. Already I caught a cold in such weather. *Blows his nose.*

MYRON *entering with stuffs:* Going home?

SAM: I'll go in bed. I caught a cold.

MYRON: Teddy Roosevelt used to say, "When you have a problem, sleep on it."

BESSIE: My Sam is no problem.

MYRON: I don't mean ... I mean he said——

BESSIE: Call me tomorrow, Sam.

SAM: I'll phone supper time. Sometime I think there's something funny about me.

MYRON *sees him out. In the following pause Caruso is heard singing within.*

BESSIE: A bargain! Second fiddle. By me he don't even play in the orchestra—a man like a mouse. Maybe she'll lay down and die 'cause he makes a living?

RALPH: Can I talk to you about something?

BESSIE: What's the matter—I'm biting you?

RALPH: It's something about Blanche.

BESSIE: Don't tell me.

RALPH: Listen now——

BESSIE: I don't wanna know.

RALPH: She's got no place to go.

BESSIE: I don't want to know.

RALPH: Mom, I love this girl. ...

BESSIE: So go knock your head against the wall.

RALPH: I want her to come here. Listen Mom, I want you to let her live here for a while.

BESSIE: You got funny ideas, my son.

RALPH: I'm as good as anyone else. Don't I have some rights in the world? Listen Mom, if I don't do something, she's going away. Why don't you do it? Why don't you let her stay here for a few weeks? Things'll pick up. Then we can——

BESSIE: Sure, sure. I'll keep her fresh on ice for a wedding day. That's what you want?

RALPH: No, I mean you should——

BESSIE: Or maybe you'll sleep here in the same bed without marriage.

JACOB *stands in his doorway, dressed.*

RALPH: Don't say that, Mom. I only mean....

BESSIE: What you mean, I know ... and what I mean I also know. Make up your mind. For your own good, Ralphie. If she dropped in the ocean I don't lift a finger.

RALPH: That's all, I suppose.

BESSIE: With me it's one thing—a boy should have respect for his own future. Go to sleep, you look tired. In the morning you'll forget.

JACOB: "Awake and sing, ye that dwell in dust, and the earth shall cast out the dead." It's cold out?

MYRON: Oh, yes.

JACOB: I'll take up Tootsie now.

MYRON *eating bread and jam:* He come on us like the wild man of Borneo, Sam. I don't think Hennie was fool enough to tell him the truth like that.

BESSIE: Myron! *A deep pause.*

RALPH: What did he say?

87

BESSIE: Never mind.

RALPH: I heard him. I heard that. You don't needa tell me.

BESSIE: Never mind.

RALPH: You trapped that guy.

BESSIE: Don't say another word.

RALPH: Just have respect? That's the idea?

BESSIE: Don't say another word. I'm boiling over ten times inside.

RALPH: You won't let Blanche here, huh. I'm not sure I want her. You put one over on that little shrimp. The cat's whiskers, Mom?

BESSIE: I'm telling you something!

RALPH: I got the whole idea. I get it so quick my head's swimming. Boy, what a laugh! I suppose you know about this, Jake?

JACOB: Yes.

RALPH: Why didn't you do something?

JACOB: I'm an old man.

RALPH: What's that got to do with the price of bonds? Sits around and lets a thing like that happen! You make me sick too.

MYRON *after a pause*: Let me say something, son.

RALPH: Take your hand away! Sit in a corner and wag your tail. Keep on boasting you went to law school for two years.

MYRON: I want to tell you——

RALPH: You never in your life had a thing to tell me.

BESSIE *bitterly*: Don't say a word. Let him, let

him run and tell Sam. Publish in the papers, give a broadcast on the radio. To him it don't matter nothing his family sits with tears pouring from the eyes. *To* JACOB: What are you waiting for? I didn't tell you twice already about the dog? You'll stand around with Caruso and make a bughouse. It ain't enough all day long. Fifty times I told you I'll break every record in the house. *She brushes past him, breaks the records, comes out.* The next time I say something you'll maybe believe it. Now maybe you learned a lesson. *Pause.*

JACOB *quietly:* Bessie, new lessons . . . not for an old dog.

MOE *enters.*

MYRON: You didn't have to do it, momma.

BESSIE: Talk better to your son, Mr. Berger! Me, I don't lay down and die for him and Poppa no more. I'll work like a nigger? For what? Wait, the day comes when you'll be punished. When it's too late you'll remember how you sucked away a mother's life. Talk to him, tell him how I don't sleep at night. *Bursts into tears and exits.*

MOE *sings:* "Good-by to all your sorrows. You never hear them talk about the war, in the land of Yama Yama. . . ."

MYRON: Yes, Momma's a sick woman, Ralphie.

RALPH: Yeah?

MOE: We'll be out of the trenches by Christmas. Putt, putt, putt . . . here, stinker. . . . *Picks up Tootsie, a small, white poodle that just then enters from the hall.* If there's reincarnation in the next life I wanna be a dog and lay in a fat lady's lap. Barrage over? How 'bout a little pinochle, Pop?

JACOB: Nnno.

RALPH *taking dog:* I'll take her up. *Conciliatory.*

JACOB: No, I'll do it. *Takes dog.*

RALPH *ashamed:* It's cold out.

JACOB: I was cold before in my life. A man sixty-seven.... *Strokes the dog.* Tootsie is my favorite lady in the house. *He slowly passes across the room and exits. A settling pause.*

MYRON: She cried all last night—Tootsie—I heard her in the kitchen like a young girl.

MOE: Tonight I could do something. I got a yen ... I don't know.

MYRON *rubbing his head:* My scalp is impoverished.

RALPH: Mom bust all his records.

MYRON: She didn't have to do it.

MOE: Tough tit! Now I can sleep in the morning. Who the hell wantsa hear a wop air his tonsils all day long!

RALPH *handling the fragment of a record:* "O Paradiso!"

MOE *gets cards:* It's snowing out, girls.

MYRON: There's no more big snows like in the old days. I think the whole world's changing. I see it, right under our very eyes. No one hardly remembers any more when we used to have gaslight and all the dishes had little fishes on them.

MOE: It's the system, girls.

MYRON: I was a little boy when it happened—the Great Blizzard. It snowed three days without a stop that time. Yes, and the horse cars stopped. A silence of death was on the city and little babies got no milk ... they say a lot of people died that year.

MOE *singing as he deals himself cards:*
"Lights are blinking while you're drinking,
  That's the place where the good fellows go.
  Good-by to all your sorrows,
  You never hear them talk about the war,
  In the land of Yama Yama
  Funicalee, funicala, funicalo. ..."

MYRON: What can I say to you, Big Boy?

RALPH: Not a damn word.

MOE *goes "ta ra ta ra" throughout.*

MYRON: I know how you feel about all those things, I know.

RALPH: Forget it.

MYRON: And your girl. ...

RALPH: Don't soft soap me all of a sudden.

MYRON: I'm not foreign born. I'm an American, and yet I never got close to you. It's an American father's duty to be his son's friend.

RALPH: Who said that—Teddy R.?

MOE *dealing cards:* You're breaking his heart, "Litvak."

MYRON: It just happened the other way. The moment I began losing my hair I just knew I was destined to be a failure in life ... and when I grew bald I was. Now isn't that funny, Big Boy?

MOE: It's a pisscutter!

MYRON: I believe in Destiny.

MOE: You get what-it-takes. Then they don't catch you with your pants down. *Sings out*: Eight of clubs....

MYRON: I really don't know. I sold jewelry on the road before I married. It's one thing to——Now here's a thing the druggist gave me. *Reads:* "The Marvel Cosmetic Girl of Hollywood is going on the air. Give this charming little radio singer a name and win five thousand dollars. If you will send——"

MOE: Your old man still believes in Santy Claus.

MYRON: Some one's got to win. The government isn't gonna allow everything to be a fake.

MOE: It's a fake. There ain't no prizes. It's a fake.

MYRON: It says——

RALPH *snatching it*: For Christ's sake, Pop, forget it. Grow up. Jake's right—everybody's crazy. It's like a zoo in this house. I'm going to bed.

MOE: In the land of Yama Yama.... *Goes on with ta ra.*

MYRON: Don't think life's easy with Momma. No, but she means for your good all the time. I tell you she does, she——

RALPH: Maybe, but I'm going to bed. *Downstairs doorbell rings violently.*

MOE (*ring*): Enemy barrage begins on sector eight seventy-five.

RALPH: That's downstairs.

MYRON: We ain't expecting anyone this hour of the night.

MOE: "Lights are blinking while you're drinking, that's the place where the good fellows go. Good-by to ta ra tara ra," etc.

RALPH: I better see who it is.

MYRON: I'll tick the button. *As he starts, the apartment doorbell begins ringing, followed by large knocking.* MYRON *goes out.*

RALPH: Who's ever ringing means it.

A loud excited voice outside.

MOE: "In the land of Yama Yama, Funicalee, funicalo, funic——

MYRON *enters followed by* SCHLOSSER *the janitor.* BESSIE *cuts in from the other side.*

BESSIE: Who's ringing like a lunatic?

RALPH: What's the matter?

MYRON: Momma....

BESSIE: Noo, what's the matter? *Downstairs bell continues.*

RALPH: What's the matter?

BESSIE: Well, well...?

MYRON: Poppa....

BESSIE: What happened?

SCHLOSSER: He shlipped maybe in de snow.

RALPH: Who?

SCHLOSSER *to* BESSIE: Your fadder fall off de roof. . . . Ja. *A dead pause.* RALPH *then runs out.*

BESSIE *dazed:* Myron. . . . Call Morty on the phone . . . call him. MYRON *starts for phone.* No. I'll do it myself. I'll . . . do it.

MYRON *exits.*

SCHLOSSER *standing stupidly:* Since I was in dis country . . . I was pudding out de ash can ,,, The snow is vet. . . .

MOE *to* SCHLOSSER: Scram.

SCHLOSSER *exits.*

BESSIE *goes blindly to the phone, fumbles and gets it.* MOE *sits quietly, slowly turning cards over, but watching her.*

BESSIE: He slipped. . . .

MOE *deeply moved:* Slipped?

BESSIE: I can't see the numbers. Make it, Moe, make it. . . .

MOE: Make it yourself. *He looks at her and slowly goes back to his game of cards with shaking hands.*

BESSIE: Riverside 7— . . . *Unable to talk she dials slowly. The dial whizzes on.*

MOE: Don't . . . make me laugh ,,, *He turns over cards.*

CURTAIN

ACT · III

ACT · III

A week later in the dining room.
MORTY, BESSIE *and* MYRON *eating.*
Sitting in the front room is MOE
marking a "dope sheet," but really
listening to the others.

BESSIE: You're sure he'll come tonight—the insurance man?

MORTY: Why not? I shtupped him a ten-dollar
bill. Everything's hot delicatessen.

BESSIE: Why must he come so soon?

MORTY: Because you had a big expense. You'll
settle once and for all. I'm a great boy for making
hay while the sun shines.

BESSIE: Stay till he'll come, Morty....

MORTY: No, I got a strike downtown. Business
don't stop for personal life. Two times already in
the past week those bastards threw stink bombs in
the showroom. Wait! We'll give them strikes—in
the kishkas we'll give them....

BESSIE: I'm a woman. I don't know about pol-
icies. Stay till he comes.

MORTY: Bessie—sweetheart, leave me live.

BESSIE: I'm afraid, Morty.

MORTY: Be practical. They made an investiga-
tion. Everybody knows Pop had an accident. Now
we'll collect.

97

MYRON: Ralphie don't know Papa left the insurance in his name.

MORTY: It's not his business. And I'll tell him.

BESSIE: The way he feels. *Enter* RALPH *into front room.* He'll do something crazy. He thinks Poppa jumped off the roof.

MORTY: Be practical, Bessie. Ralphie will sign when I tell him. Everything is peaches and cream.

BESSIE: Wait for a few minutes....

MORTY: Look, I'll show you in black on white what the policy says. *For God's sake, leave me live! Angrily exits to kitchen.*

In parlor, MOE *speaks to* RALPH *who is reading a letter.*

MOE: What's the letter say?

RALPH: Blanche won't see me no more, she says. I couldn't care very much, she says. If I didn't come like I said.... She'll phone before she leaves.

MOE: She don't know about Pop?

RALPH: She won't ever forget me she says. Look what she sends me ... a little locket on a chain ... if she calls I'm out.

MOE: You mean it?

RALPH: For a week I'm trying to go in his room. I guess he'd like me to have it, but I can't....

MOE: Wait a minute! *Crosses over.* They're trying to rook you—a freeze-out.

RALPH: Who?

MOE: That bunch stuffin' their gut with hot

pastrami. Morty in particular. Jake left the insurance—three thousand dollars—for you.

RALPH: For me?

MOE: Now you got wings, kid. Pop figured you could use it. That's why....

RALPH: That's why what?

MOE: It ain't the only reason he done it.

RALPH: He done it?

MOE: You think a breeze blew him off?

HENNIE *enters and sits.*

RALPH: I'm not sure what I think.

MOE: The insurance guy's coming tonight. Morty "shtupped" him.

RALPH: Yeah?

MOE: I'll back you up. You're dead on your feet. Grab a sleep for yourself.

RALPH: No!

MOE: Go on! *Pushes boy into room.*

SAM *whom* MORTY *has sent in for the paper:* Morty wants the paper.

HENNIE: So?

SAM: You're sitting on it. *Gets paper.* We could go home now, Hennie! Leon is alone by Mrs. Strasberg a whole day.

HENNIE: Go on home if you're so anxious. A full tub of diapers is waiting.

SAM: Why should you act this way?

HENNIE: 'Cause there's no bones in ice cream. Don't touch me....

SAM: Please, what's the matter....

MOE: She don't like you. Plain as the face on your nose. . . .

SAM: To me, my friend, you talk a foreign language.

MOE: A quarter you're lousy. *Sam exits.* Gimme a buck, I'll run it up to ten.

HENNIE: Don't do me no favors.

MOE: Take a chance. *Stopping her as she crosses to doorway.*

HENNIE: I'm a pushover.

MOE: I say lotsa things. You don't know me.

HENNIE: I know you—when you knock 'em down you're through.

MOE *sadly:* You still don't know me.

HENNIE: I know what goes in your wise-guy head.

MOE: Don't run away. . . . I ain't got hydrophobia. Wait. I want to tell you. . . . I'm leaving.

HENNIE: Leaving?

MOE: Tonight. Already packed.

HENNIE: Where?

MORTY *as he enters followed by the others:* My car goes through snow like a dose of salts.

BESSIE: Hennie, go eat. . . .

MORTY: Where's Ralphie?

MOE: In his new room. *Moves into dining room.*

MORTY: I didn't have a piece of hot pastrami in my mouth for years.

BESSIE: Take a sandwich, Hennie. You didn't

eat all day.... *At window:* A whole week it rained cats and dogs.

MYRON: Rain, rain, go away. Come again some other day. *Puts shawl on her.*

MORTY: Where's my gloves?

SAM *sits on stool:* I'm sorry the old man lays in the rain.

MORTY: Personally, Pop was a fine man. But I'm a great boy for an honest opinion. He had enough crazy ideas for a regiment.

MYRON: Poppa never had a doctor in his whole life....

Enter RALPH.

MORTY: He had Caruso. Who's got more from life?

BESSIE: Who's got more? ...

MYRON: And Marx he had.

MYRON *and* BESSIE *sit on sofa.*

MORTY: Marx! Some say Marx is the new God today. Maybe I'm wrong. Ha ha ha.... Personally I counted my ten million last night.... I'm sixteen cents short. So tomorrow I'll go to Union Square and yell no equality in the country! Ah, it's a new generation.

RALPH: You said it!

MORTY: What's the matter, Ralphie? What are you looking funny?

RALPH: I hear I'm left insurance and the man's coming tonight.

MORTY: Poppa didn't leave no insurance for you.

RALPH: What?

MORTY: In your name he left it—but not for you.

RALPH: It's my name on the paper.

MORTY: Who said so?

RALPH *to his mother*: The insurance man's coming tonight?

MORTY: What's the matter?

RALPH: I'm not talking to you. *To his mother*: Why?

BESSIE: I don't know why.

RALPH: He don't come in this house tonight.

MORTY: That's what *you* say.

RALPH: I'm not talking to you, Uncle Morty, but I'll tell you, too, he don't come here tonight when there's still mud on a grave. *To his mother*: Couldn't you give the house a chance to cool off?

MORTY: Is this a way to talk to your mother?

RALPH: Was that a way to talk to your father?

MORTY: Don't be so smart with me, Mr. Ralph Berger!

RALPH: Don't be so smart with *me*.

MORTY: What'll you do? I say he's coming tonight. Who says no?

MOE *suddenly, from the background*: Me.

MORTY: Take a back seat, Axelrod. When you're in the family——

MOE: I got a little document here. *Produces*

paper. I found it under his pillow that night. A guy who slips off a roof don't leave a note before he does it.

MORTY *starting for* MOE *after a horrified silence:* Let me see this note.

BESSIE: Morty, don't touch it!

MOE: Not if you crawled.

MORTY: It's a fake. Poppa wouldn't——

MOE: Get the insurance guy here and we'll see how—— *The bell rings.* Speak of the devil. . . . Answer it, see what happens. MORTY *starts for the ticker.*

BESSIE: Morty, don't!

MORTY *stopping:* Be practical, Bessie.

MOE: Sometimes you don't collect on suicides if they know about it.

MORTY: You should let. . . . You should let him. . . .

A pause in which ALL *seem dazed. Bell rings insistently.*

MOE: Well, we're waiting.

MORTY: Give me the note.

MOE: I'll give you the head off your shoulders.

MORTY: Bessie, you'll stand for this? *Points to* RALPH. Pull down his pants and give him with a strap.

RALPH *as bell rings again:* How about it?

BESSIE: Don't be crazy. It's not my fault. Morty said he should come tonight. It's not nice so soon. I didn't——

MORTY: I said it? Me?

BESSIE: Who then?

MORTY: You didn't sing a song in my ear a whole week to settle quick?

BESSIE: I'm surprised, Morty, you're a big liar.

MYRON: Momma's telling the truth, she is!

MORTY: Lissen. In two shakes of a lamb's tail, we'll start a real fight and then nobody won't like nobody. Where's my fur gloves? I'm going downtown. *To* SAM: You coming? I'll drive you down.

HENNIE *to* SAM, *who looks questioningly at her:* Don't look at me. Go home if you want.

SAM: If you're coming soon, I'll wait.

HENNIE: Don't do me any favors. Night and day he pesters me.

MORTY: You made a cushion——sleep!

SAM: I'll go home. I know ... to my worst enemy I don't wish such a life——

HENNIE: Sam, keep quiet.

SAM *quietly; sadly:* No more free speech in America? *Gets his hat and coat.* I'm a lonely person. Nobody likes me.

MYRON: I like you, Sam.

HENNIE *going to him gently; sensing the end:* Please go home, Sam. I'll sleep here.... I'm tired and nervous. Tomorrow I'll come home. I love you ... I mean it. *She kisses him with real feeling.*

SAM: I would die for you....

SAM *looks at her. Tries to say something, but his*

voice chokes up with a mingled feeling. He turns and leaves the room.

MORTY: A bird in the hand is worth two in the bush. Remember I said it. Good night. *Exits after* SAM.

HENNIE *sits depressed.* BESSIE *goes up and looks at the picture calendar again.* MYRON *finally breaks the silence.*

MYRON: Yesterday a man wanted to sell me a saxophone with pearl buttons. But I——

BESSIE: It's a beautiful picture. In this land, nobody works. . . . Nobody worries. . . . Come to bed, Myron. *Stops at the door, and says to* RALPH: Please don't have foolish ideas about the money.

RALPH: Let's call it a day.

BESSIE: It belongs for the whole family. You'll get your teeth fixed——

RALPH: And a pair of black and white shoes?

BESSIE: Hennie needs a vacation. She'll take two weeks in the mountains and I'll mind the baby.

RALPH: I'll take care of my own affairs.

BESSIE: A family needs for a rainy day. Times is getting worse. Prospect Avenue, Dawson, Beck Street—every day furniture's on the sidewalk.

RALPH: Forget it, Mom.

BESSIE: Ralphie, I worked too hard all my years to be treated like dirt. It's no law we should be stuck together like Siamese twins. Summer shoes you didn't have, skates you never had, but I bought a new dress every week. A lover I kept—Mr.

Gigolo! Did I ever play a game of cards like Mrs. Marcus? Or was Bessie Berger's children always the cleanest on the block?! Here I'm not only the mother, but also the father. The first two years I worked in a stocking factory for six dollars while Myron Berger went to law school. If I didn't worry about the family who would? On the calendar it's a different place, but here without a dollar you don't look the world in the eye. Talk from now to next year—this is life in America.

RALPH: Then it's wrong. It don't make sense. If life made you this way, then it's wrong!

BESSIE: Maybe you wanted me to give up twenty years ago. Where would you be now? You'll excuse my expression—a bum in the park!

RALPH: I'm not blaming you, Mom. Sink or swim—I see it. But it can't stay like this.

BESSIE: My foolish boy....

RALPH: No, I see every house lousy with lies and hate. He said it, Grandpa— Brooklyn hates the Bronx. Smacked on the nose twice a day. But boys and girls can get ahead like that, Mom. We don't want life printed on dollar bills, Mom!

BESSIE: So go out and change the world if you don't like it.

RALPH: I will! And why? 'Cause life's different in my head. Gimme the earth in two hands. I'm strong. There...hear him? The air mail off to Boston. Day or night, he flies away, a job to do. That's us and it's no time to die.

AWAKE AND SING!

The airplane sound fades off as MYRON *gives alarm clock to* BESSIE *which she begins to wind.*

BESSIE: "Mom, what does she know? She's old-fashioned!" But I'll tell you a big secret: My whole life I wanted to go away too, but with children a woman stays home. A fire burned in *my* heart too, but now it's too late. I'm no spring chicken. The clock goes and Bessie goes. Only my machinery can't be fixed. *She lifts a button: the alarm rings on the clock; she stops it, says "Good night" and exits.*

MYRON: I guess I'm no prize bag....

BESSIE *from within:* Come to bed, Myron.

MYRON *tears page off calendar:* Hmmm.... *Exits to her.*

RALPH: Look at him, draggin' after her like an old shoe.

MOE: Punch drunk. *Phone rings.* That's for me. *At phone.* Yeah?... Just a minute. *To Ralph:* Your girl...

RALPH: Jeez, I don't know what to say to her.

MOE: Hang up?

RALPH *slowly takes phone.*

RALPH: Hello.... Blanche, I wish.... I don't know what to say. . . . Yes . . . Hello? . . . *Puts phone down.* She hung up on me . . .

MOE: Sorry?

RALPH: No girl means anything to me until. . . .

MOE: Till when?

RALPH: Till I can take care of her. Till we

don't look out on an airshaft. Till we can take the world in two hands and polish off the dirt.

MOE: That's a big order.

RALPH: Once upon a time I thought I'd drown to death in bolts of silk and velour. But I grew up these last few weeks. Jake said a lot.

MOE: Your memory's okay?

RALPH: But take a look at this. *Brings armful of books from* JACOB's *room—dumps them on table.* His books, I got them too—the pages ain't cut in half of them.

MOE: Perfect.

RALPH: Does it prove something? Damn tootin'! A ten-cent nail-file cuts them. Uptown, downtown, I'll read them on the way. Get a big lamp over the bed. *Picks up one.* My eyes are good. *Puts book in pocket.* Sure, inventory tomorrow. Coletti to Driscoll to Berger—that's how we work. It's a team down the warehouse. Driscoll's a show-off, a wiseguy, and Joe talks pigeons day and night. But they're like me, looking for a chance to get to first base too. Joe razzed me about my girl. But he don't know why. I'll tell him. Hell, he might tell me something I don't know. Get teams together all over. Spit on your hands and get to work. And with enough teams together maybe we'll get steam in the warehouse so our fingers don't freeze off. Maybe we'll fix it so life won't be printed on dollar bills.

MOE: Graduation Day.

RALPH *starts for door of his room, stops:* Can I have... Grandpa's note?

MOE: Sure you want it?

RALPH: Please— MOE *gives it.* It's blank!

MOE *taking note back and tearing it up:* That's right.

RALPH: Thanks! *Exits.*

MOE: The kid's a fighter! *To* HENNIE: Why you crying?

HENNIE: I never cried in my life. *She is now.*

MOE *starts for door. Stops:* You told Sam you love him....

HENNIE: If I'm sore on life, why take it out on him?

MOE: You won't forget me to your dyin' day— I was the first guy. Part of your insides. You won't forget. I wrote my name on you—indelible ink!

HENNIE: One thing I won't forget—how you left me crying on the bed like I was two for a cent!

MOE: Listen, do you think——

HENNIE: Sure. Waits till the family goes to the open air movie. He brings me perfume.... He grabs my arms——

MOE: You won't forget me!

HENNIE: How you left the next week?

MOE: So I made a mistake. For chris' sake, don't act like the Queen of Roumania!

HENNIE: Don't make me laugh!

MOE: What the hell do you want, my head on a plate?! Was my life so happy? Chris', my old man

109

was a bum. I supported the whole damn family—
five kids and Mom. When they grew up they beat
it the hell away like rabbits. Mom died. I went to
the war; got clapped down like a bedbug; woke
up in a room without a leg. What the hell do you
think, anyone's got it better than you? I never
had a home either. I'm lookin' too!

HENNIE: So what?!

MOE: So you're it—you're home for me, a place
to live! That's the whole parade, sickness, eating
out your heart! Sometimes you meet a girl—she
stops it—that's love. . . . So take a chance! Be with
me, Paradise. What's to lose?

HENNIE: My pride!

MOE *grabbing her:* What do you want? Say the
word—I'll tango on a dime. Don't gimme ice
when your heart's on fire!

HENNIE: Let me go! *He stops her.*

MOE: WHERE?!!

HENNIE: What do you want, Moe, what do you
want?

MOE: You!

HENNIE: You'll be sorry you ever started——

MOE: You!

HENNIE: Moe, lemme go—— *Trying to leave:*
I'm getting up early—lemme go.

MOE: No! . . . I got enough fever to blow the
whole damn town to hell. *He suddenly releases her
and half stumbles backwards. Forces himself to*

quiet down. You wanna go back to him? Say the word. I'll know what to do. . . .

HENNIE *helplessly:* Moe, I don't know what to say.

MOE: Listen to me.

HENNIE: What?

MOE: Come away. A certain place where it's moonlight and roses. We'll lay down, count stars. Hear the big ocean making noise. You lay under the trees. Champagne flows like—— *Phone rings.*
MOE *finally answers the telephone:* Hello? . . . Just a minute. *Looks at* HENNIE.

HENNIE: Who is it?

MOE: Sam.

HENNIE *starts for phone, but changes her mind:* I'm sleeping. . . .

MOE *in phone:* She's sleeping. . . . *Hangs up. Watches* HENNIE *who slowly sits.* He wants you to know he got home O.K. . . . What's on your mind?

HENNIE: Nothing.

MOE: Sam?

HENNIE: They say it's a palace on those Havana boats.

MOE: What's on your mind?

HENNIE *trying to escape:* Moe, I don't care for Sam—I never loved him——

MOE: But your kid—?

HENNIE: All my life I waited for this minute.

MOE *holding her:* Me too. Made believe I was

talkin' just bedroom golf, but you and me forever was what I meant! Christ, baby, there's one life to live! Live it!

HENNIE: Leave the baby?

MOE: Yeah!

HENNIE: I can't....

MOE: You can!

HENNIE: No....

MOE: But you're not sure!

HENNIE: I don't know.

MOE: Make a break or spend the rest of your life in a coffin.

HENNIE: Oh God, I don't know where I stand.

MOE: Don't look up there. Paradise, you're on a big boat headed south. No more pins and needles in your heart, no snake juice squirted in your arm. The whole world's green grass and when you cry it's because you're happy.

HENNIE: Moe, I don't know....

MOE: Nobody knows, but you do it and find out. When you're scared the answer's zero.

HENNIE: You're hurting my arm.

MOE: The doctor said it—cut off your leg to save your life! And they done it—one thing to get another.

Enter RALPH.

RALPH: I didn't hear a word, but do it, Hennie, do it!

MOE: Mom can mind the kid. She'll go on forever, Mom. We'll send money back, and Easter eggs.

RALPH: I'll be here.

MOE: Get your coat . . . get it.

HENNIE: Moe!

MOE: I know . . . but get your coat and hat and kiss the house good-by.

HENNIE: The man I love. . . . MYRON *entering*. I left my coat in Mom's room. *Exits*.

MYRON: Don't wake her up, Beauty. Momma fell asleep as soon as her head hit the pillow. I can't sleep. It was a long day. Hmmm. *Examines his tongue in buffet mirror:* I was reading the other day a person with a thick tongue is feeble-minded. I can do anything with my tongue. Make it thick, flat. No fruit in the house lately. Just a lone apple. *He gets apple and paring knife and starts paring.* Must be something wrong with me —I say I won't eat but I eat. HENNIE *enters dressed to go out.* Where you going, little Red Riding Hood?

HENNIE: Nobody knows, Peter Rabbit.

MYRON: You're looking very pretty tonight. You were a beautiful baby too. 1910, that was the year you was born. The same year Teddy Roosevelt come back from Africa.

HENNIE: Gee, Pop; you're such a funny guy.

MYRON: He was a boisterous man, Teddy. Good night. *He exits, paring apple.*

RALPH: When I look at him, I'm sad. Let me die like a dog, if I can't get more from life.

HENNIE: Where?

RALPH: Right here in the house! My days won't be for nothing. Let Mom have the dough. I'm twenty-two and kickin'! I'll get along. Did Jake die for us to fight about nickels? No! "Awake and sing," he said. Right here he stood and said it. The night he died, I saw it like a thunderbolt! I saw he was dead and I was born! I swear to God, I'm one week old! I want the whole city to hear it— fresh blood, arms. We got 'em. We're glad we're living.

MOE: I wouldn't trade you for two pitchers and an outfielder. Hold the fort!

RALPH: So long.

MOE: So long.

They go and RALPH *stands full and strong in the doorway seeing them off as the curtain slowly falls.*

CURTAIN

WAITING FOR
LEFTY

NOTE

THIS PLAY was first presented by the Group Theatre at the Longacre Theatre on the evening of March 26th, 1935, with the following members of the Group Theatre Acting Company:

Played by

Fatt . . . . RUSSELL COLLINS
Joe . . . . LEWIS LEVERETT
Edna . . . . RUTH NELSON
Miller . . . . GERRIT KRABER
Fayette . . . . RUSSELL COLLINS
Irv . . . . WALTER COY
Florrie . . . . PAULA MILLER
Sid . . . . HERBERT RATNER
Clayton . . . . BOB LEWIS
Agate Keller . . . . ELIA KAZAN
Henchman . . . . ABNER BIBERMAN
Secretary . . . . DOROTHY PATTEN
Actor . . . . WILLIAM CHALLEE
Reilly . . . . RUSSELL COLLINS
Dr. Barnes . . . . ROMAN BOHNEN
Dr. Benjamin . . . . CLIFFORD ODETS
A Man . . . . GEORGE HELLER
Voices—SAM ROLAND, LEE J. COBB, WENDELL KEITH PHILLIPS, HARRY STONE, BERNARD ZANVILLE.

As the curtain goes up we see a bare stage. On it are sitting six or seven men in a semi-circle. Lolling against the proscenium down left is a young man chewing a tooth-pick: a gunman. A fat man of porcine appearance is talking directly to the audience. In other words he is the head of a union and the men ranged behind him are a committee of workers. They are now seated in interesting different attitudes and present a wide diversity of type, as we shall soon see. The fat man is hot and heavy under the collar, near the end of a long talk, but not too hot: he is well fed and confident. His name is HARRY FATT.

FATT: You're so wrong I ain't laughing. Any guy with eyes to read knows it. Look at the textile strike—out like lions and in like lambs. Take the San Francisco tie-up—starvation and broken heads. The steel boys wanted to walk out too, but they changed their minds. It's the trend of the times,

3

that's what it is. All we workers got a good man behind us now. He's top man of the country—looking out for our interests—the man in the White House is the one I'm referrin' to. That's why the times ain't ripe for a strike. He's working day and night—

VOICE *from the audience:* For who? *The* GUN-MAN *stirs himself.*

FATT: For you! The records prove it. If this was the Hoover régime, would I say don't go out, boys? Not on your tintype! But things is different now. You read the papers as well as me. You know it. And that's why I'm against the strike. Because we gotta stand behind the man who's standin' behind us! The whole country——

ANOTHER VOICE: Is on the blink! *The* GUNMAN *looks grave.*

FATT: Stand up and show yourself, you damn red! Be a man, let's see what you look like! *Waits in vain.* Yellow from the word go! Red and yellow makes a dirty color, boys. I got my eyes on four or five of them in the union here. What the hell'll they do for you? Pull you out and run away when trouble starts. Give those birds a chance and they'll have your sisters and wives in the whore houses, like they done in Russia. They'll tear Christ off his bleeding cross. They'll wreck your homes and throw your babies in the river. You think that's bunk? Read the papers! Now listen, we can't stay here all night. I gave you the facts in the case. You boys got hot suppers to go to and——

ANOTHER VOICE: Says you!

GUNMAN: Sit down, Punk!

ANOTHER VOICE: Where's Lefty? *Now this question is taken up by the others in unison.* FATT *pounds with gavel.*

FATT: That's what I wanna know. Where's your pal, Lefty? You elected him chairman—where the hell did he disappear?

VOICES: We want Lefty! Lefty! Lefty!

FATT *pounding*: What the hell is this—a circus? You got the committee here. This bunch of cowboys you elected. *Pointing to man on extreme right end.*

MAN: Benjamin.

FATT: Yeah, Doc Benjamin. *Pointing to other men in circle in seated order:* Benjamin, Miller, Stein, Mitchell, Phillips, Keller. It ain't my fault Lefty took a run-out powder. If you guys——

A GOOD VOICE: What's the committee say?

OTHERS: The committee! Let's hear from the committee! FATT *tries to quiet the crowd, but one of the seated men suddenly comes to the front. The* GUNMAN *moves over to center stage, but* FATT *says:*

FATT: Sure, let him talk. Let's hear what the red boys gotta say!

Various shouts are coming from the audience. FATT *insolently goes back to his seat in the middle*

5

of the circle. He sits on his raised platform and re-
lights his cigar. The GUNMAN *goes back to his post.*
JOE, *the new speaker, raises his hand for quiet.*
Gets it quickly. He is sore.

JOE: You boys know me. I ain't a red boy one
bit! Here I'm carryin' a shrapnel that big I picked
up in the war. And maybe I don't know it when
it rains! Don't tell me red! You know what
we are? The black and blue boys! We been
kicked around so long we're black and blue from
head to toes. But I guess anyone who says straight
out he don't like it, he's a red boy to the leaders
of the union. What's this crap about goin' home
to hot suppers? I'm asking to your faces how
many's got hot suppers to go home to? Anyone
who's sure of his next meal, raise your hand! A
certain gent sitting behind me can raise them both.
But not in front here! And that's why we're talking strike—to get a living wage!

VOICE: Where's Lefty?

JOE: I honest to God don't know, but he didn't
take no run-out powder. That Wop's got more
guts than a slaughter house. Maybe a traffic jam
got him, but he'll be here. But don't let this red
stuff scare you. Unless fighting for a living scares
you. We gotta make up our minds. My wife made
up my mind last week, if you want the truth. It's
plain as the nose on Sol Feinberg's face we need
a strike. There's us comin' home every night—
eight, ten hours on the cab. "God," the wife says,

"eighty cents ain't money—don't buy beans almost. You're workin' for the company," she says to me, "Joe! you ain't workin' for me or the family no more!" She says to me, "If you don't start...."

I · JOE AND EDNA

The lights fade out and a white spot picks out the playing space within the space of seated men. The seated men are very dimly visible in the outer dark, but more prominent is FATT *smoking his cigar and often blowing the smoke in the lighted circle.*

A tired but attractive woman of thirty comes into the room, drying her hands on an apron. She stands there sullenly as JOE *comes in from the other side, home from work. For a moment they stand and look at each other in silence.*

JOE: Where's all the furniture, honey?

EDNA: They took it away. No installments paid.

JOE: When?

EDNA: Three o'clock.

JOE: They can't do that.

EDNA: Can't? They did it.

JOE: Why, the palookas, we paid three-quarters.

EDNA: The man said read the contract.

JOE: We must have signed a phoney....

EDNA: It's a regular contract and you signed it.

JOE: Don't be so sour, Edna.... *Tries to embrace her.*

8

EDNA: Do it in the movies, Joe—they pay Clark Gable big money for it.

JOE: This is a helluva house to come home to. Take my word!

EDNA: Take MY word! Whose fault is it?

JOE: Must you start that stuff again?

EDNA: Maybe you'd like to talk about books?

JOE: I'd like to slap you in the mouth!

EDNA: No you won't.

JOE *sheepish:* Jeez, Edna, you get me sore some time....

EDNA: But just look at me—I'm laughing all over!

JOE: Don't insult me. Can I help it if times are bad? What the hell do you want me to do, jump off a bridge or something?

EDNA: Don't yell. I just put the kids to bed so they won't know they missed a meal. If I don't have Emmy's shoes soled tomorrow, she can't go to school. In the meantime let her sleep.

JOE: Honey, I rode the wheels off the chariot today. I cruised around five hours without a call. It's conditions.

EDNA: Tell it to the A & P!

JOE: I booked two-twenty on the clock. A lady with a dog was lit...she gave me a quarter tip by mistake. If you'd only listen to me—we're rolling in wealth.

EDNA: Yeah? How much?

9

WAITING FOR LEFTY

JOE: I had "coffee and—" in a beanery. *Hands her silver coins.* A buck four.

EDNA: The second month's rent is due tomorrow.

JOE: Don't look at me that way, Edna.

EDNA: I'm looking through you, not at you. . . . Everything was gonna be so ducky! A cottage by the waterfall, roses in Picardy. You're a four-star-bust! If you think I'm standing for it much longer, you're crazy as a bedbug.

JOE: I'd get another job if I could. There's no work—you know it.

EDNA: I only know we're at the bottom of the ocean.

JOE: What can I do?

EDNA: Who's the man in the family, you or me?

JOE: That's no answer. Get down to brass tacks. Christ, gimme a break, too! A coffee cake and java all day. I'm hungry, too, Babe. I'd work my fingers to the bone if—

EDNA: I'll open a can of salmon.

JOE: Not now. Tell me what to do!

EDNA: I'm not God!

JOE: Jeez, I wish I was a kid again and didn't have to think about the next minute.

EDNA: But you're not a kid and you do have to think about the next minute. You got two blondie kids sleeping in the next room. They need food and clothes. I'm not mentioning anything else—But we're stalled like a flivver in the snow. For five years I laid awake at night listening to my heart pound. For God's sake, do something, Joe, get wise. Maybe get your buddies together, maybe go on strike for better money. Poppa did it during the war and they won out. I'm turning into a sour old nag.

JOE *defending himself*: Strikes don't work!

EDNA: Who told you?

JOE: Besides that means not a nickel a week while we're out. Then when it's over they don't take you back.

EDNA: Suppose they don't! What's to lose?

JOE: Well, we're averaging six-seven dollars a week now.

EDNA: That just pays for the rent.

JOE: That is something, Edna.

EDNA: It isn't. They'll push you down to three and four a week before you know it. Then you'll say, "That's somethin'," too!

JOE: There's too many cabs on the street, that's the whole damn trouble.

EDNA: Let the company worry about that, you big fool! If their cabs didn't make a profit, they'd take them off the streets. Or maybe you think they're in business just to pay Joe Mitchell's rent!

JOE: You don't know a-b-c, Edna.

EDNA: I know this—your boss is making suckers outa you boys every minute. Yes, and suckers out of all the wives and the poor innocent kids who'll grow up with crooked spines and sick bones. Sure, I see it in the papers, how good orange juice is for kids. But dammit our kids get colds one on top of the other. They look like little ghosts. Betty never saw a grapefruit. I took her to the store last week and she pointed to a stack of grapefruits. "What's that!" she said. My God, Joe—the world is supposed to be for all of us.

JOE: You'll wake them up.

EDNA: I don't care, as long as I can maybe wake you up.

JOE: Don't insult me. One man can't make a strike.

EDNA: Who says one? You got hundreds in your rotten union!

JOE: The Union ain't rotten.

EDNA: No? Then what are they doing? Collecting dues and patting your back?

JOE: They're making plans.

EDNA: What kind?

JOE: They don't tell us.

EDNA: It's too damn bad about you. They don't tell little Joey what's happening in his bitsie witsie union. What do you think it is—a ping pong game?

JOE: You know they're racketeers. The guys at the top would shoot you for a nickel.

EDNA: Why do you stand for that stuff?

JOE: Don't you wanna see me alive?

EDNA *after a deep pause:* No . . . I don't think I do, Joe. Not if you can lift a finger to do something about it, and don't. No, I don't care.

WAITING FOR LEFTY

JOE: Honey, you don't understand what—

EDNA: And any other hackie that won't fight
... let them all be ground to hamburger!

JOE: It's one thing to—

EDNA: Take your hand away! Only they don't
grind me to little pieces! I got different plans.
Starts to take off her apron.

JOE: Where are you going?

EDNA: None of your business.

JOE: What's up your sleeve?

EDNA: My arm'd be up my sleeve, darling, if I
had a sleeve to wear. *Puts neatly folded apron on
back of chair.*

JOE: Tell me!

EDNA: Tell you what?

JOE: Where are you going?

EDNA: Don't you remember my old boy friend?

JOE: Who?

EDNA: Bud Haas. He still has my picture in his
watch. He earns a living.

JOE: What the hell are you talking about?

EDNA: I heard worse than I'm talking about.

JOE: Have you seen Bud since we got married?

EDNA: Maybe.

JOE: If I thought . . . . *He stands looking at her.*

EDNA: See much? Listen, boy friend, if you
think I won't do this it just means you can't see
straight.

JOE: Stop talking bull!

EDNA: This isn't five years ago, Joe.

13

WAITING FOR LEFTY

JOE: You mean you'd leave me and the kids?

EDNA: I'd leave *you* like a shot!

JOE: No. . . .

EDNA: Yes!

JOE *turns away, sitting in a chair with his back to her. Outside the lighted circle of the playing stage we hear the other seated members of the strike committee. "She will . . . she will . . . it happens that way," etc. This group should be used throughout for various comments, political, emotional and as general chorus. Whispering. . . . The fat boss now blows a heavy cloud of smoke into the scene.*

JOE *finally:* Well, I guess I ain't got a leg to stand on.

EDNA: No?

JOE *suddenly mad:* No, you lousy tart, no! Get the hell out of here. Go pick up that bull-thrower on the corner and stop at some cushy hotel downtown. He's probably been coming here every morning and laying you while I hacked my guts out!

EDNA: You're crawling like a worm!

JOE: You'll be crawling in a minute.

EDNA: You don't scare me that much! *Indicates a half inch on her finger.*

JOE: This is what I slaved for!

EDNA: Tell it to your boss!

JOE: He don't give a damn for you or me!

EDNA: That's what I say.

JOE: Don't change the subject!

WAITING FOR LEFTY

EDNA: This is the subject, the EXACT SUBJECT! Your boss makes this subject. I never saw him in my life, but he's putting ideas in my head a mile a minute. He's giving your kids that fancy disease called the rickets. He's making a jelly-fish outa you and putting wrinkles in my face. This is the subject every inch of the way! He's throwing me into Bud Haas' lap. When in hell will you get wise——

JOE: I'm not so dumb as you think! But you are talking like a Red.

EDNA: I don't know what that means. But when a man knocks you down you get up and kiss his fist! You gutless piece of boloney.

JOE: One man can't——

EDNA *with great joy:* I don't say one man! I say a hundred, a thousand, a whole million, I say. But start in your own union. Get those hack boys together! Sweep out those racketeers like a pile of dirt! Stand up like men and fight for the crying kids and wives. Goddammit! I'm tired of slavery and sleepless nights.

JOE *with her:* Sure, sure! ...

EDNA: Yes. Get brass toes on your shoes and know where to kick!

JOE *suddenly jumping up and kissing his wife full on the mouth:* Listen, Edna. I'm goin' down to 174th Street to look up Lefty Costello. Lefty was saying the other day.... *He suddenly stops.* How about this Haas guy?

15

WAITING FOR LEFTY

EDNA: Get out of here!

JOE: I'll be back! *Runs out.*

For a moment EDNA *stands triumphant.*

There is a blackout and when the regular lights come up, JOE MITCHELL *is concluding what he has been saying:*

JOE: You guys know this stuff better than me. We gotta walk out! *Abruptly he turns and goes back to his seat and blackout.*

BLACKOUT

II . LAB ASSISTANT EPISODE

> *Discovered:* MILLER, *a lab assist-*
> *ant, looking around; and* FAY-
> ETTE, *an industrialist.*

FAY: Like it?

MILLER: Very much. I've never seen an office like this outside the movies.

FAY: Yes, I often wonder if interior decorators and bathroom fixture people don't get all their ideas from Hollywood. Our country's extraordinary that way. Soap, cosmetics, electric refrigerators—just let Mrs. Consumer know they're used by the Crawfords and Garbos—more volume of sale than one plant can handle!

MILL: I'm afraid it isn't that easy, Mr. Fayette.

FAY: No, you're right—gross exaggeration on my part. Competition is cut-throat today. Markets up flush against a stone wall. The astronomers had better hurry—open Mars to trade expansion.

MILL: Or it will be just too bad!

FAY: Cigar?

MILL: Thank you, don't smoke.

FAY: Drink?

MILL: Ditto, Mr. Fayette.

FAY: I like sobriety in my workers...the trained ones, I mean. The Pollacks and niggers, they're better drunk—keeps them out of mischief. Wondering why I had you come over?

MILL: If you don't mind my saying—very much.

FAY *patting him on the knee*: I like your work.

MILL: Thanks.

FAY: No reason why a talented young man like yourself shouldn't string along with us—a growing concern. Loyalty is well repaid in our organization. Did you see Siegfried this morning?

MILL: He hasn't been in the laboratory all day.

FAY: I told him yesterday to raise you twenty dollars a month. Starts this week.

MILL: You don't know how happy my wife'll be.

FAY: Oh, I can appreciate it. *He laughs.*

MILL: Was that all, Mr. Fayette?

FAY: Yes, except that we're switching you to laboratory A tomorrow. Siegfried knows about it. That's why I had you in. The new work is very important. Siegfried recommended you very highly as a man to trust. You'll work directly under Dr. Brenner. Make you happy?

MILL: Very. He's an important chemist!

FAY *leaning over seriously*: We think so, Miller. We think so to the extent of asking you to stay within the building throughout the time you work with him.

MILL: You mean sleep and eat in?

FAY: Yes. . . .

WAITING FOR LEFTY

MILL: It can be arranged.

FAY: Fine. You'll go far, Miller.

MILL: May I ask the nature of the new work?

FAY *looking around first*: Poison gas. . . .

MILL: Poison!

FAY: Orders from above. I don't have to tell you from where. New type poison gas for modern warfare.

MILL: I see.

FAY: You didn't know a new war was that close, did you?

MILL: I guess I didn't.

FAY: I don't have to stress the importance of absolute secrecy.

MILL: I understand!

FAY: The world is an armed camp today. One match sets the whole world blazing in forty-eight hours. Uncle Sam won't be caught napping!

MILL *addressing his pencil*: They say 12 million men were killed in that last one and 20 million more wounded or missing.

FAY: That's not our worry. If big business went sentimental over human life there wouldn't be big business of any sort!

MILL: My brother and two cousins went in the last one.

FAY: They died in a good cause.

MILL: My mother says "no!"

FAY: She won't worry about you this time. You're too valuable behind the front.

WAITING FOR LEFTY

MILL: That's right.

FAY: All right, Miller. See Siegfried for further orders.

MILL: You should have seen my brother—he could ride a bike without hands. . . .

FAY: You'd better move some clothes and shaving tools in tomorrow. Remember what I said—you're with a growing organization.

MILL: He could run the hundred yards in 9:8 flat. . . .

FAY: Who?

MILL: My brother. He's in the Meuse-Argonne Cemetery. Momma went there in 1926. . . .

FAY: Yes, those things stick. How's your handwriting, Miller, fairly legible?

MILL: Fairly so.

FAY: Once a week I'd like a little report from you.

MILL: What sort of report?

FAY: Just a few hundred words once a week on Dr. Brenner's progress.

MILL: Don't you think it might be better coming from the Doctor?

FAY: I didn't ask you that.

MILL: Sorry.

FAY: I want to know what progress he's making, the reports to be purely confidential—between you and me.

MILL: You mean I'm to watch him?

FAY: Yes!

MILL: I guess I can't do that. . . .

FAY: Thirty a month raise . . .

MILL: You said twenty. . . .

FAY: Thirty!

MILL: Guess I'm not built that way.

FAY: Forty. . . .

MILL: Spying's not in my line, Mr. Fayette!

FAY: You use ugly words, Mr. Miller!

MILL: For ugly activity? Yes!

FAY: Think about it, Miller. Your chances are excellent. . . .

MILL: No.

FAY: You're doing something for your country. Assuring the United States that when those goddam Japs start a ruckus we'll have offensive weapons to back us up! Don't you read your newspapers, Miller?

MILL: Nothing but Andy Gump.

FAY: If you were on the inside you'd know I'm talking cold sober truth! Now, I'm not asking you to make up your mind on the spot. Think about it over your lunch period.

MILL: No. . . .

FAY: Made up your mind already?

MILL: Afraid so.

FAY: You understand the consequences?

MILL: I lose my raise——

Simultaneously: { MILL: And my job!
FAY: And your job!
MILL: You misunderstand——

WAITING FOR LEFTY

MILL: Rather dig ditches first!

FAY: That's a big job for foreigners.

MILL: But sneaking—and making poison gas—that's for Americans?

FAY: It's up to you.

MILL: My mind's made up.

FAY: No hard feelings?

MILL: Sure hard feelings! I'm not the civilized type, Mr. Fayette. Nothing suave or sophisticated about me. Plenty of hard feelings! Enough to want to bust you and all your kind square in the mouth!

Does exactly that.

BLACKOUT

III · THE YOUNG HACK AND HIS GIRL

Opens with girl and brother. FLORENCE *waiting for* SID *to take her to a dance.*

FLOR: I gotta right to have something out of life. I don't smoke, I don't drink. So if Sid wants to take me to a dance, I'll go. Maybe if you was in love you wouldn't talk so hard.

IRV: I'm saying it for your good.

FLOR: Don't be so good to me.

IRV: Mom's sick in bed and you'll be worryin' her to the grave. She don't want that boy hanging around the house and she don't want you meeting him in Crotona Park.

FLOR: I'll meet him anytime I like!

IRV: If you do, yours truly'll take care of it in his own way. With just one hand, too!

FLOR: Why are you all so set against him?

IRV: Mom told you ten times—it ain't him. It's that he ain't got nothing. Sure, we know he's serious, that he's stuck on you. But that don't cut no ice.

FLOR: Taxi drivers used to make good money.

IRV: Today they're makin' five and six dollars a week. Maybe you wanta raise a family on that. Then you'll be back here living with us again and

23

WAITING FOR LEFTY

I'll be supporting two families in one. Well...
over my dead body.

FLOR: Irv, I don't care—I love him!

IRV: You're a little kid with half-baked ideas!

FLOR: I stand there behind the counter the whole
day. I think about him—

IRV: If you thought more about Mom it would
be better.

FLOR: Don't I take care of her every night when
I come home? Don't I cook supper and iron your
shirts and ... you give me a pain in the neck, too.
Don't try to shut me up! I bring a few dollars
in the house, too. Don't you see I want something
else out of life. Sure, I want romance, love, babies.
I want everything in life I can get.

IRV: You take care of Mom and watch your
step!

FLOR: And if I don't?

IRV: Yours truly'll watch it for you!

FLOR: You can talk that way to a girl. . . .

IRV: I'll talk that way to your boy friend, too,
and it won't be with words! Florrie, if you had
a pair of eyes you'd see it's for your own good
we're talking. This ain't no time to get married.
Maybe later—

FLOR: "Maybe Later" never comes for me,
though. Why don't we send Mom to a hospital?
She can die in peace there instead of looking at
the clock on the mantelpiece all day.

IRV: That needs money. Which we don't have!

24

FLOR: Money, Money, Money!

IRV: Don't change the subject.

FLOR: This is the subject!

IRV: You gonna stop seeing him? *She turns away.* Jesus, kiddie, I remember when you were a baby with curls down your back. Now I gotta stand here yellin' at you like this.

FLOR: I'll talk to him, Irv.

IRV: When?

FLOR: I asked him to come here tonight. We'll talk it over.

IRV: Don't get soft with him. Nowadays is no time to be soft. You gotta be hard as a rock or go under.

FLOR: I found that out. There's the bell. Take the egg off the stove I boiled for Mom. Leave us alone, Irv.

SID *comes in—the two men look at each other for a second.* IRV *exits.*

SID *enters:* Hello, Florrie.

FLOR: Hello, Honey. You're looking tired.

SID: Naw, I just need a shave.

FLOR: Well, draw your chair up to the fire and I'll ring for brandy and soda ... like in the movies.

SID: If this was the movies I'd bring a big bunch of roses.

FLOR: How big?

SID: Fifty or sixty dozen—the kind with long, long stems—big as that....

FLOR: You dope....

25

WAITING FOR LEFTY

SID: Your Paris gown is beautiful.

FLOR *acting grandly*: Yes, Percy, velvet panels are coming back again. Madame La Farge told me today that Queen Marie herself designed it.

SID: Gee ... !

FLOR: Every princess in the Balkans is wearing one like this. *Poses grandly.*

SID: Hold it. *Does a nose camera—thumbing nose and imitating grinding of camera with other hand.*

Suddenly she falls out of the posture and swiftly goes to him, to embrace him, to kiss him with love. Finally:

SID: You look tired, Florrie.

FLOR: Naw, I just need a shave. *She laughs tremorously.*

SID: You worried about your mother?

FLOR: No.

SID: What's on your mind?

FLOR: The French and Indian War.

SID: What's on your mind?

FLOR: I got us on my mind, Sid. Night and day, Sid!

SID: I smacked a beer truck today. Did I get hell! I was driving along thinking of US, too. You don't have to say it—I know what's on your mind. I'm rat poison around here.

FLOR: Not to me. . . .

SID: I know to who . . . and I know why. I don't blame them. We're engaged now for three years. . . .

WAITING FOR LEFTY

FLOR: That's a long time....

SID: My brother Sam joined the navy this morning—get a break that way. They'll send him down to Cuba with the hootchy-kootchy girls. He don't know from nothing, that dumb basket ball player!

FLOR: Don't you do that.

SID: Don't you worry, I'm not the kind who runs away. But I'm so tired of being a dog, Baby, I could choke. I don't even have to ask what's going on in your mind. I know from the word go, 'cause I'm thinking the same things, too.

FLOR: It's yes or no—nothing in between.

SID: The answer is no—a big electric sign looking down on Broadway!

FLOR: We wanted to have kids....

SID: But that sort of life ain't for the dogs which is us. Christ, Baby! I get like thunder in my chest when we're together. If we went off together I could maybe look the world straight in the face, spit in its eye like a man should do. Goddamit, it's trying to be a man on the earth. Two in life together.

FLOR: But something wants us to be lonely like that—crawling alone in the dark. Or they want us trapped.

SID: Sure, the big shot money men want us like that.

FLOR: Highly insulting us——

SID: Keeping us in the dark about what is wrong with us in the money sense. They got the power an mean to be damn sure they keep it. They know if they give in just an inch, all the dogs like us will be down on them together—an ocean knocking them to hell and back and each singing cuckoo with stars coming from their nose and ears. I'm not raving, Florrie——

FLOR: I know you're not, I know.

SID: I don't have the words to tell you what I feel. I never finished school....

FLOR: I know....

SID: But it's relative, like the professors say. We worked like hell to send him to college—my kid brother Sam, I mean—and look what he done—joined the navy! The damn fool don't see the cards is stacked for all of us. The money man dealing himself a hot royal flush. Then giving you and me a phoney hand like a pair of tens or something. Then keep on losing the pots 'cause the cards is stacked against you. Then he says, what's the matter you can't win—no stuff on the ball, he says to you. And kids like my brother believe it 'cause they don't know better. For all their education, they don't know from nothing.

But wait a minute! Don't he come around and say to you—this millionaire with a jazz band—listen Sam or Sid or what's-your-name, you're no good, but here's a chance. The whole world'll know who you are. Yes sir, he says, get up on that ship and fight those bastards who's making the world a lousy place to live in. The Japs, the Turks, the Greeks. Take this gun—kill the slobs like a real hero, he says, a real American. Be a hero!

And the guy you're poking at? A real louse, just like you, 'cause they don't let him catch more than a pair of tens, too. On that foreign soil he's a guy like me and Sam, a guy who wants his baby like you and hot sun on his face! They'll teach Sam to point the guns the wrong way, that dumb basket ball player!

FLOR: I got a lump in my throat, Honey.

SID: You and me—we never even had a room to sit in somewhere.

FLOR: The park was nice...

SID: In Winter? The hallways...I'm glad we never got together. This way we don't know what we missed.

FLOR *in a burst:* Sid, I'll go with you—we'll get a room somewhere.

SID: Naw...they're right. If we can't climb higher than this together—we better stay apart.

FLOR: I swear to God I wouldn't care.

SID: You would, you would—in a year, two years, you'd curse the day. I seen it happen.

FLOR: Oh, Sid....

SID: Sure I know. We got the blues, Babe—the 1935 blues. I'm talkin' this way 'cause I love you. If I didn't, I wouldn't care....

FLOR: We'll work together, we'll—

WAITING FOR LEFTY

SID: How about the backwash? Your family needs your nine bucks. My family——

FLOR: I don't care for them!

SID: You're making it up, Florrie. Little Florrie Canary in a cage.

FLOR: Don't make fun of me.

SID: I'm not, Baby.

FLOR: Yes, you're laughing at me.

SID: I'm not.

They stand looking at each other, unable to speak. Finally, he turns to a small portable phonograph and plays a cheap, sad, dance tune. He makes a motion with his hand; she comes to him. They begin to dance slowly. They hold each other tightly, almost as though they would merge into each other. The music stops, but the scratching record continues to the end of the scene. They stop dancing. He finally unlooses her clutch and seats her on the couch, where she sits, tense and expectant.

SID: Hello, Babe.

FLOR: Hello. *For a brief time they stand as though in a dream.*

SID *finally:* Good-by, Babe.

He waits for an answer, but she is silent. They look at each other.

SID: Did you ever see my Pat Rooney imitation? *He whistles Rosy O'Grady and soft shoes to it. Stops. He asks:*

WAITING FOR LEFTY

SID: Don't you like it?

FLOR *finally:* No. *Buries her face in her hands. Suddenly he falls on his knees and buries his face in her lap.*

BLACKOUT

IV · LABOR SPY EPISODE

FATT: You don't know how we work for you. Shooting off your mouth won't help. Hell, don't you guys ever look at the records like me? Look in your own industry. See what happened when the hacks walked out in Philly three months ago! Where's Philly? A thousand miles away? An hour's ride on the train.

VOICE: Two hours!!

FATT: Two hours . . . what the hell's the difference. Let's hear from someone who's got the practical experience to back him up. Fellers, there's a man here who's seen the whole parade in Philly, walked out with his pals, got knocked down like the rest—and blacklisted after they went back. That's why he's here. He's got a mighty interestin' word to say. *Announces:* TOM CLAYTON!

As CLAYTON *starts up from the audience,* FATT *gives him a hand which is sparsely followed in the audience.* CLAYTON *comes forward.*

Fellers, this is a man with practical strike experience—Tom Clayton from little ole Philly.

CLAYTON *a thin, modest individual:* Fellers, I don't mind your booing. If I thought it would help us hacks get better living conditions, I'd let you walk all over me, cut me up to little pieces. I'm one of you myself. But what I wanna say is that

32

WAITING FOR LEFTY

Harry Fatt's right. I only been working here in the big town five weeks, but I know conditions just like the rest of you. You know how it is— don't take long to feel the sore spots, no matter where you park.

CLEAR VOICE *from audience:* Sit down!

CLAYTON: But Fatt's right. Our officers is right. The time ain't ripe. Like a fruit don't fall off the tree until it's ripe.

CLEAR VOICE: Sit down, you fruit!

FATT *on his feet:* Take care of him, boys.

VOICE *in audience, struggling:* No one takes care of me.

Struggle in house and finally the owner of the voice runs up on stage, says to speaker:

SAME VOICE: Where the hell did you pick up that name! Clayton! This rat's name is Clancy, from the old Clancys, way back! Fruit! I almost wet myself listening to that one!

FATT *gunman with him:* This ain't a barn! What the hell do you think you're doing here!

SAME VOICE: Exposing a rat!

FATT: You can't get away with this. Throw him the hell outa here.

VOICE *preparing to stand his ground:* Try it yourself.... When this bozo throws that slop around. You know who he is? That's a company spy.

FATT: Who the hell are you to make—

VOICE: I paid dues in this union for four years,

33

WAITING FOR LEFTY

that's who's me! I gotta right and this pussy-footed rat ain't coming in here with ideals like that. You know his record. Lemme say it out——

FATT: You'll prove all this or I'll bust you in every hack outfit in town!

VOICE: I gotta right. I gotta right. Looka *him,* he don't say boo!

CLAYTON: You're a liar and I never seen you before in my life!

VOICE: Boys, he spent two years in the coal fields breaking up any organization he touched. Fifty guys he put in jail. He's ranged up and down the east coast—shipping, textiles, steel—he's been in everything you can name. Right now——

CLAYTON: That's a lie!

VOICE: Right now he's working for that Bergman outfit on Columbus Circle who furnishes rats for any outfit in the country before, during, and after strikes.

The man who is the hero of the next episode goes down to his side with other committee men.

CLAYTON: He's trying to break up the meeting, fellers!

VOICE: We won't search you for credentials....

CLAYTON: I got nothing to hide. Your own secretary knows I'm straight.

VOICE: Sure. Boys, you know who this sonova-bitch is?

CLAYTON: I never seen you before in my life!!

VOICE: Boys, I slept with him in the same

34

bed sixteen years. HE'S MY OWN LOUSY BROTHER!!

FATT *after pause:* Is this true? *No answer from* CLAYTON.

VOICE *to* CLAYTON: Scram, before I break your neck!

CLAYTON *scrams down center aisle.* VOICE *says, watching him:*

Remember his map—he can't change that—Clancy!

Standing in his place says:

Too bad you didn't know about this, Fatt! *After a pause.* The Clancy family tree is bearing nuts!

Standing isolated clear on the stage is the hero of the next episode.

BLACKOUT

V · THE YOUNG ACTOR

A New York theatrical producer's office. Present are a stenographer and a young actor. She is busy typing; he, waiting with card in hand.

STEN: He's taking a hot bath . . . says you should wait.

PHILIPS *the actor:* A bath did you say? Where?

STEN: See that door? Right through there— leads to his apartment.

PHIL: Through there?

STEN: Mister, he's laying there in a hot perfumed bath. Don't say I said it.

PHIL: You don't say!

STEN: An oriental den he's got. Can you just see this big Irishman burning Chinese punk in the bedroom? And a big old rose canopy over his casting couch. . . .

PHIL: What's that—casting couch?

STEN: What's that? You from the sticks?

PHIL: I beg your pardon?

STEN *rolls up her sleeves, makes elaborate deaf and dumb signs:* No from side walkies of New Yorkie . . . savvy?

36

PHIL: Oh, you're right. Two years of dramatic stock out of town. One in Chicago.

STEN: Don't tell him, Baby Face. He wouldn't know a good actor if he fell over him in the dark. Say you had two years with the Group, two with the Guild.

PHIL: I'd like to get with the Guild. They say——

STEN: He won't know the difference. Don't say I said it!

PHIL: I really did play with Watson Findlay in "Early Birds."

STEN *withering him*: Don't tell him!

PHIL: He's a big producer, Mr. Grady. I wish I had his money. Don't you?

STEN: Say, I got a clean heart, Mister. I love my fellow man! *About to exit with typed letters.* Stick around—Mr. Philips. You might be the type. If you were a woman——

PHIL: Please. Just a minute . . . please . . . I need the job.

STEN: Look at him!

PHIL: I mean . . . I don't know what buttons to push, and you do. What my father used to say— we had a gas station in Cleveland before the crash —"Know what buttons to push," Dad used to say, "and you'll go far."

STEN: You can't push me, Mister! I don't ring right these last few years!

37

WAITING FOR LEFTY

PHIL: We don't know where the next meal's coming from. We——

STEN: Maybe . . . I'll lend you a dollar?

PHIL: Thanks very much: it won't help.

STEN: One of the old families of Virginia? Proud?

PHIL: Oh, not that. You see, I have a wife. We'll have our first baby next month . . . so . . . a dollar isn't much help.

STEN: Roped in?

PHIL: I love my wife!

STEN: Okay, you love her! Excuse me! You married her. Can't support her. No . . . not blaming you. But you're fools, all you actors. Old and young! Watch you parade in and out all day. You still got apples in your cheeks and pins for buttons. But in six months you'll be like them—putting on an act: Phoney strutting "pishers"—that's French for dead codfish! It's not their fault. Here you get like that or go under. What kind of job is this for an adult man!

PHIL: When you have to make a living——

STEN: I know, but——

PHIL: Nothing else to do. If I could get something else——

STEN: You'd take it!

PHIL: Anything!

STEN: Telling me! With two brothers in my hair!

Mr. Grady now enters; played by FATT. Mr. Brown sent this young man over.

WAITING FOR LEFTY

GRADY: Call the hospital: see how Boris is. *She assents and exits.*

PHIL: Good morning, Mr. Grady....

GRADY: The morning is lousy!

PHIL: Mr. Brown sent me. *Hands over card.*

GRADY: I heard that once already.

PHIL: Excuse me....

GRADY: What experience?

PHIL: Oh, yes....

GRADY: Where?

PHIL: Two years in stock, sir. A year with the Goodman Theatre in Chicago....

GRADY: That all?

PHIL *abashed*: Why no...with the Theatre Guild...I was there....

GRADY: Never saw you in a Guild show!

PHIL: On the road, I mean...understudying Mr. Lunt...

GRADY: What part? *Philips can not answer.* You're a lousy liar, son.

PHIL: I did....

GRADY: You don't look like what I want. Can't understand that Brown. Need a big man to play a soldier. Not a lousy soldier left on Broadway! All in pictures, and we get the nances! *Turns to work on desk.*

PHIL *immediately playing the soldier*: I was in the ROTC in college...Reserve Officers' Training Corps. We trained twice a week....

GRADY: Won't help.

PHIL: With real rifles. *Waits*. Mr. Grady, I weigh a hundred and fifty-five!

GRADY: How many years back? Been eating regular since you left college?

PHIL *very earnestly*: Mr. Grady, I could act this soldier part. I could build it up and act it. Make it up——

GRADY: Think I run a lousy acting school around here?

PHIL: Honest to God I could! I need the job— that's why I could do it! I'm strong. I know my business! YOU'll get an A-1 performance. Because I need this job! My wife's having a baby in a few weeks. We need the money. Give me a chance!

GRADY: What do I care if you can act it! I'm sorry about your baby. Use your head, son. Tank Town stock is different. Here we got investments to be protected. When I sink fifteen thousand in a show I don't take chances on some youngster. We cast to type!

PHIL: I'm an artist! I can——

GRADY: That's your headache. Nobody interested in artists here. Get a big bunch for a nickel on any corner. Two flops in a row on this lousy street nobody loves you—only God, and He don't count. We protect investments: we cast to type. Your face and height we want, not your soul, son. And Jesus Christ himself couldn't play a soldier in this

WAITING FOR LEFTY

show ... with all his talent. *Crosses himself in quick repentance for this remark.*

PHIL: Anything ... a bit, a walk-on?

GRADY: Sorry: small cast. *Looking at papers on his desk.* You try Russia, son. I hear its hot stuff over there.

PHIL: Stage manager? Assistant?

GRADY: All filled, sonny. *Stands up; crumples several papers from the desk.* Better luck next time.

PHIL: Thanks. ...

GRADY: Drop in from time to time. *Crosses and about to exit.* You never know when something —— *The* STENOGRAPHER *enters with papers to put on desk.* What did the hospital say?

STEN: He's much better, Mr. Grady.

GRADY: Resting easy?

STEN: Dr. Martel said Boris is doing even better than he expected.

GRADY: A damn lousy operation!

STEN: Yes. ...

GRADY *belching*: Tell the nigger boy to send up a bromo seltzer.

STEN: Yes, Mr. Grady. *He exits.* Boris wanted lady friends.

PHIL: What?

STEN: So they operated ... poor dog!

PHIL: A dog?

STEN: His Russian Wolf Hound! They do the same to you, but you don't know it! *Suddenly:* Want advice? In the next office, don't let them

41

see you down in the mouth. They don't like it—makes them shiver.

PHIL: You treat me like a human being. Thanks. . . .

STEN: You're human!

PHIL: I used to think so.

STEN: He wants a bromo for his hangover. *Goes to door.* Want that dollar?

PHIL: It won't help much.

STEN: One dollar buys ten loaves of bread, Mister. Or one dollar buys nine loaves of bread and one copy of The Communist Manifesto. Learn while you eat. Read while you run. . . .

PHIL: Manifesto? What's that? *Takes dollar.* What is that, what you said. . . . Manifesto?

STEN: Stop off on your way out—I'll give you a copy. From Genesis to Revelation, Comrade Philips! "And I saw a new earth and a new heaven; for the first earth and the first heaven were passed away; and there was no more sea."

PHIL: I don't understand that. . . .

STEN: I'm saying the meek shall not inherit the earth!

PHIL: No?

STEN: The MILITANT! Come out in the light, Comrade.

BLACKOUT

VI · INTERNE EPISODE

Dr. Barnes, an elderly distinguished man, is speaking on the telephone. He wears a white coat.

DR. BARNES: No, I gave you my opinion twice. You outvoted me. You did this to Dr. Benjamin yourself. That is why you can tell him yourself.

Hangs up phone, angrily. As he is about to pour himself a drink from a bottle on the table, a knock is heard.

BARNES: Who is it?

BENJAMIN *without*: Can I see you a minute, please?

BARNES *hiding the bottle*: Come in, Dr. Benjamin, come in.

BENJ: It's important—excuse me—they've got Leeds up there in my place—He's operating on Mrs. Lewis—the historectomy—it's my job. I washed up, prepared ... they told me at the last minute. I don't mind being replaced, Doctor, but Leeds is a damn fool! He shouldn't be permitted——

BARNES *dryly*: Leeds is the nephew of Senator Leeds.

BENJ: He's incompetent as hell.

BARNES *obviously changing subject, picks up lab.*

WAITING FOR LEFTY

jar: They're doing splendid work in brain surgery these days. This is a very fine specimen. . . .

BENJ: I'm sorry, I thought you might be interested.

BARNES *still examining jar*: Well, I am, young man, I am! Only remember it's a charity case!

BENJ: Of course. They wouldn't allow it for a second, otherwise.

BARNES: Her life is in danger?

BENJ: Of course! You know how serious the case is!

BARNES: Turn your gimlet eyes elsewhere, Doctor. Jigging around like a cricket on a hot grill won't help. Doctors don't run these hospitals. He's the Senator's nephew and there he stays.

BENJ: It's too bad.

BARNES: I'm not calling you down either. *Plopping down jar suddenly.* Goddammit, do you think it's my fault?

BENJ *about to leave*: I know . . . I'm sorry.

BARNES: Just a minute. Sit down.

BENJ: Sorry, I can't sit.

BARNES: Stand then!

BENJ *sits*: Understand, Dr. Barnes, I don't mind being replaced at the last minute this way, but . . . well, this flagrant bit of class distinction—because she's poor——

BARNES: Be careful of words like that—"class distinction." Don't belong here. Lots of energy,

WAITING FOR LEFTY

you brilliant young men, but idiots. Discretion! Ever hear that word?

BENJ: Too radical?

BARNES: Precisely. And some day like in Germany, it might cost you your head.

BENJ: Not to mention my job.

BARNES: So they told you?

BENJ: Told me what?

BARNES: They're closing Ward C next month. I don't have to tell you the hospital isn't self supporting. Until last year that board of trustees met deficits. . . . You can guess the rest. At a board meeting Tuesday, our fine feathered friends discovered they couldn't meet the last quarter's deficit —a neat little sum well over $100,000. If the hospital is to continue at all, its damn——

BENJ: Necessary to close another charity ward!

BARNES: So they say. . . . *A wait.*

BENJ: But that's not all?

BARNES *ashamed*: Have to cut down on staff too. . . .

BENJ: That's too bad. Does it touch me?

BARNES: Afraid it does.

BENJ: But after all I'm top man here. I don't mean I'm better than others, but I've worked harder.

BARNES: And shown more promise. . . .

BENJ: I always supposed they'd cut from the bottom first.

BARNES: Usually.

BENJ: But in this case?

BARNES: Complications.

BENJ: For instance? BARNES *hesitant.*

BARNES: I like you, Benjamin. It's one ripping shame.

BENJ: I'm no sensitive plant—what's the answer?

BARNES: An old disease, malignant, tumescent. We need an anti-toxin for it.

BENJ: I see.

BARNES: What?

BENJ: I met that disease before—at Harvard first.

BARNES: You have seniority here, Benjamin.

BENJ: But I'm a Jew! BARNES *nods his head in agreement.* BENJ *stands there a moment and blows his nose.*

BARNES *blows his nose*: Microbes!

BENJ: Pressure from above?

BARNES: Don't think Kennedy and I didn't fight for you!

BENJ: Such discrimination, with all those wealthy brother Jews on the board?

BARNES: I've remarked before—doesn't seem to be much difference between wealthy Jews and rich Gentiles. Cut from the same piece!

BENJ: For myself I don't feel sorry. My parents gave up an awful lot to get me this far. They ran a little dry goods shop in the Bronx until their pitiful savings went in the crash last year. Poppa's peddling neckties.... Saul Ezra Benjamin—a man who's read Spinoza all his life.

BARNES: Doctors don't run medicine in this country. The men who know their jobs don't run anything here, except the motormen on trolley cars. I've seen medicine change—plenty—anesthesia, sterilization—but not because of rich men— in *spite* of them! In a rich man's country your true self's buried deep. Microbes! Less.... Vermin! See this ankle, this delicate sensitive hand? Four hundred years to breed that. Out of a revolutionary background! Spirit of '76! Ancestors froze at Valley Forge! What's it all mean! Slops! The honest workers were sold out then, in '76. The Constitution's for rich men then and now. Slops! *The phone rings.*

BARNES *angrily*: Dr. Barnes. *Listens a moment, looks at Benjamin.* I see. *Hangs up, turns slowly to the younger Doctor.* They lost your patient.

BENJ *stands solid with the shock of this news but finally hurls his operation gloves to the floor.*

BARNES: That's right...that's right. Young, hot, go and do it! I'm very ancient, fossil, but life's ahead of you, Dr. Benjamin, and when you fire the first shot say, "This one's for old Doc Barnes!" Too much dignity—bullets. Don't shoot vermin! Step on them! If I didn't have an invalid daughter——

BARNES *goes back to his seat, blows his nose in silence*: I have said my piece, Benjamin.

WAITING FOR LEFTY

BENJ: Lots of things I wasn't certain of. Many things these radicals say... you don't believe theories until they happen to you.

BARNES: You lost a lot today, but you won a great point.

BENJ: Yes, to know I'm right? To really begin believing in something? Not to say, "What a world!", but to say, "Change the world!" I wanted to go to Russia. Last week I was thinking about it —the wonderful opportunity to do good work in their socialized medicine——

BARNES: Beautiful, beautiful!

BENJ: To be able to work——

BARNES: Why don't you go? I might be able——

BENJ: Nothing's nearer what I'd like to do!

BARNES: Do it!

BENJ: No! Our work's here—America! I'm scared.... What future's ahead, I don't know. Get some job to keep alive—maybe drive a cab—and study and work and learn my place——

BARNES: And step down hard!

BENJ: Fight! Maybe get killed, but goddam! We'll go ahead! *Benjamin stands with clenched fist raised high.*

BLACKOUT

48

AGATE: LADIES AND GENTLEMEN, and don't let anyone tell you we ain't got some ladies in this sea of upturned faces! Only they're wearin' pants. Well, maybe I don't know a thing; maybe I fell outa the cradle when I was a kid and ain't been right since—you can't tell!

VOICE: Sit down, cockeye!

AGATE: Who's paying you for those remarks, Buddy?—Moscow Gold? Maybe I got a *glass eye*, but it come from working in a factory at the age of eleven. They hooked it out because they didn't have a shield on the works. But I wear it like a medal 'cause it tells the world where I belong— deep down in the working class! We had delegates in the union there—all kinds of secretaries and treasurers ... walkin' delegates, but not with blisters on their feet! Oh no! On their fat little ass from sitting on cushions and raking in mazuma. SECRETARY *and* GUNMAN *remonstrate in words and actions here.* Sit down, boys. I'm just sayin' that about unions in general. I know it ain't true here! Why no, our officers is all aces. Why, I seen our own secretary Fatt walk outa his way not to step on a cockroach. No boys, don't think——

FATT *breaking in*: You're out of order!

AGATE *to audience*: Am I outa order?

49

WAITING FOR LEFTY

ALL: No, no. Speak. Go on, etc.

AGATE: Yes, our officers is all aces. But I'm a member here—and no experience in Philly either! Today I couldn't wear my union button. The damnest thing happened. When I take the old coat off the wall, I see she's smoking. I'm a sonovagun if the old union button isn't on fire! Yep, the old celluloid was makin' the most god-awful stink: the landlady come up and give me hell! You know what happened?—that old union button just blushed itself to death! Ashamed! Can you beat it?

FATT: Sit down, Keller! Nobody's interested!

AGATE: Yes they are!

GUNMAN: Sit down like he tells you!

AGATE *continuing to audience*: And when I finish——

His speech is broken by FATT *and* GUNMAN *who physically handle him. He breaks away and gets to other side of stage. The two are about to make for him when some of the committee men come forward and get in between the struggling parties.* AGATE's *shirt has been torn.*

AGATE *to audience*: What's the answer, boys? The answer is, if we're reds because we wanna strike, then we take over their salute too! Know how they do it? *Makes Communist salute.* What is it? An uppercut! The good old uppercut to the chin! Hell, some of us boys ain't even got a shirt to our backs. What's the boss class tryin' to do—make a nudist colony outa us?

WAITING FOR LEFTY

The audience laughs and suddenly AGATE *comes to the middle of the stage so that the other cabmen back him up in a strong clump.*

AGATE: Don't laugh! Nothing's funny! This is your life and mine! It's skull and bones every incha the road! Christ, we're dyin' by inches! For what? For the debutant-ees to have their sweet comin' out parties in the Ritz! Poppa's got a daughter she's gotta get her picture in the papers. Christ, they make 'em with our blood. Joe said it. Slow death or fight. It's war!

Throughout this whole speech AGATE *is backed up by the other six workers, so that from their activity it is plain that the whole group of them are saying these things. Several of them may take alternate lines out of this long last speech.*

You Edna, God love your mouth! Sid and Florrie, the other boys, old Doc Barnes—fight with us for right! It's war! Working class, unite and fight! Tear down the slaughter house of our old lives! Let freedom really ring.

These slick slobs stand here telling us about bogeymen. That's a new one for the kids—the reds is bogeymen! But the man who got me food in 1932, he called me Comrade! The one who picked me up where I bled—he called me Comrade too! What are we waiting for. . . . Don't wait for Lefty! He might never come. Every minute——

This is broken into by a man who has dashed

WAITING FOR LEFTY

*up the center aisle from the back of the house.
He runs up on stage, says:*

MAN: Boys, they just found Lefty!

OTHERS: What? What? What?

SOME: Shhh.... Shhh....

MAN: They found Lefty....

AGATE: Where?

MAN: Behind the car barns with a bullet in his head!

AGATE *crying*: Hear it, boys, hear it? Hell, listen to me! Coast to coast! HELLO AMERICA! HELLO. WE'RE STORMBIRDS OF THE WORKING - CLASS. WORKERS OF THE WORLD.... OUR BONES AND BLOOD! And when we die they'll know what we did to make a new world! Christ, cut us up to little pieces. We'll die for what is right! put fruit trees where our ashes are!

To audience: Well, what's the answer?

ALL: STRIKE!

AGATE: LOUDER!

ALL: STRIKE!

AGATE and OTHERS on Stage: AGAIN!

ALL: STRIKE, STRIKE, STRIKE!!!

CURTAIN

NOTES FOR PRODUCTION

The background of the episodes, a strike meeting, is not an excuse. Each of the committeemen shows in his episode the crucial moment of his life which brought him to this very platform. The dramatic structure on which the play has been built is simple but highly effective. The form used is the old black-face minstrel form of chorus, end men, specialty men and interlocutor.

In Fatt's scenes before the "Spy Exposé," mention should again be made of Lefty's tardiness. Sitting next to Fatt in the center of the circle is a little henchman who sits with his back to the audience. On the other side of Fatt is Lefty's empty chair. This is so indicated by Fatt when he himself asks: "Yeah, where's your chairman?"

Fatt, of course, represents the capitalist system throughout the play. The audience should constantly be kept aware of him, the ugly menace which hangs over the lives of all the people who act out their own dramas. Perhaps he puffs smoke into the spotted playing space; perhaps during the action of a playlet he might insolently walk in and around the unseeing players. It is possible that some highly gratifying results can be achieved by the imaginative use of this character.

53

The strike committee on the platform during the acting out of the playlets should be used as chorus. Emotional, political, musical, they have in them possibilities of various comments on the scenes. This has been indicated once in the script in the place where Joe's wife is about to leave him. In the climaxes of each scene, slogans might very effectively be used—a voice coming out of the dark. Such a voice might announce at the appropriate moments in the "Young Interne's" scene that the USSR is the only country in the world where Anti-Semitism is a crime against the State.

Do not hesitate to use music wherever possible. It is very valuable in emotionally stirring an audience.

TILL THE DAY
I DIE

NOTE

On the Original Production

THIS PLAY was first presented by the Group Theatre at the Longacre Theatre on the evening of March 26th, 1935, with the following members of the Group Theatre Acting Company:

	Played by
Karl Tausig	WALTER COY
Baum	ELIA KAZAN
Ernst Tausig	ALEXANDER KIRKLAND
Tillie	MARGARET BARKER
Zelda	EUNICE STODDARD
Detective Popper	LEE J. COBB
Martin, an orderly	BOB LEWIS
Another Orderly	HARRY STONE
Captain Schlegel	LEWIS LEVERETT
Adolph	HERBERT RATNER
Zeltner	DAVID KORTCHMAR
Schlupp	RUSSELL COLLINS
Edsel Peltz	WILLIAM CHALLEE
1st Storm Trooper	SAMUEL ROLAND
2nd Storm Trooper	HARRY STONE
3rd Storm Trooper	GERRIT KRABER
4th Storm Trooper	ABNER BIBERMAN
Boy	WENDELL KEITH PHILLIPS

Old Man ....George Heller
Other Prisoners...Elia Kazan, David Kortch-
                            mar, Paul Morrison
Major Duhring ....Roman Bohnen
Frau Duhring ....Dorothy Patten
1st Detective ....Gerrit Kraber
2nd Detective ....David Kortchmar
Secretary ....George Heller
Arno ....Samuel Roland
Stieglitz ....Lee Martin
Julius ....Bernard Zanville
Women........Ruth Nelson, Paula Miller

The action takes place in present-day Berlin.

scene 1—*An underground room.*
scene 2—*Office room in the Columbia Brown
            house.*
scene 3—*Barracks room, Brown house.*
scene 4—*Office room.*
scene 5—*Tilly's room.*
scene 6—*An underground meeting room.*
scene 7—*Carl's room.*

"till the day i die" *was suggested by a letter
from Germany printed in* "The New Masses."

The production was directed by Cheryl Crawford
The scenery was designed by Alexander Chertoff
from suggestions by Paul Morrison.

SCENE · I

A small room underground in Berlin today.

A small man with a rueful face, named BAUM, *is silently operating a hectograph machine. Watching him are the two brothers* ERNST *and* CARL TAUSIG. *Downstage at a long littered table sits an alert girl who is concentrated on work before her. Her name is* TILLY WESTERMANN. *The two brothers watch the operating machine for quite some time.* CARL *finally picks up a leaflet which has just come from the machine. Scans it, replaces it finally.*

CARL: How long will this stencil hold out?

BAUM *singing out the answer*: Another hundred.

ERNST: That's plenty. This particular leaflet's going to make some of our Nazi's friends perspire once it gets into the workers' hands. Workers might like to know the American embargo on German goods has increased 50% in the last six months. They might like to know wages are down one third and vital foods are up seventy-five per cent.

4

TILLY *without looking up*: Stop loafing, comrades.

ERNST *humor ugly*: She says that to a man who hasn't slept for thirty hours.

CARL: Listen, Dodo, you better take care. Just out of a sick bed, and——

ERNST: Good as new. I could swing you around my finger.

CARL *laughing*: Try it. *They spar with good nature.*

TILLY: Comrades! Stop loafing!

CARL: That's right. *Picks up leaflets.* How many of these do I take?

ERNST: Two hundred. Get them to Zeltner. He'll take care of distribution.

CARL: Listen Ernst, I hate to say it, I don't trust Zeltner.

TILLY *suddenly looks up*, BAUM *turns his head.*

ERNST: Why don't you trust Zeltner?

CARL: He is too damn brave, too damn willing to die for what he calls "The Cause," too damn downright curious.

ERNST: In the last analysis maybe just romantic.

CARL: He wanted to know this address. Is that romantic?

ERNST: He asked?

CARL: This morning. I told him Berlin's a big city.

TILLY: Did he press the point?

CARL: No, but his knuckles went white around the pencil.

ERNST: We are prepared to move on a moment's notice. Baum's removing the machine as soon as he is finished. In the meantime deliver this package to Zeltner.

CARL: Why take a chance?

ERNST: When we see what he does with this package we'll know where we stand.

CARL *seriously*: I see.

BAUM: I used to be a peaceful man who planted tulips.

ERNST: Get going Carl, the back streets.

TILLY *not looking up*: All Comrades to be referred to by first names. Please remember to spread the word.

BAUM *sings "Oh Tannenbaum."*

CARL: I don't suppose you and Tilly could come to Frieda's to hear some Bach tonight.

ERNST: With all this work?

CARL: Do you know the trio hasn't met for five months?

BAUM *sings*: My father hated music.

ERNST: My fingers are stiff as boards.

BAUM: The day he died a six-piece band accompanied him right to the cemetery.

ERNST: Not to have touched a violin for six months? Incredible!

CARL: See you tomorrow.

ERNST *stopping him*: Wait a minute, Carl. I

6

know what's on your mind. Every time we say good-by we both think, "When will we meet again? ... What will tomorrow bring? ... Is this the last time together?"

CARL *trying to jest*: Look, a mind-reader.

ERNST: You must be careful Carl.

CARL: I know how you feel.

ERNST: You've got an awful hot head. You mustn't ever lose your temper when you find yourself in a jam.

CARL *laughing*: Don't worry about your little brother, he is slippery as an eel.

BAUM: Did you ever eat a pickled eel?

ERNST: Be careful.

CARL: Sure. *The brothers grip hands and look at each other.* Know what I do? When I walk in the streets I sing. That makes them say "He's above board, he can't be doing underground work." But they don't know I'm singing because I know where we'll be some day. When I sing——

TILLY: You sing yourself right out of here, comrade. Right this minute.

CARL *laughing:* Correctmente, as the Spaniards say. Adios.

ERNST: Adios.

TILLY: And pull the door tight.

BAUM: Don't take no wooden money. CARL *exits.*

ERNST: I wouldn't like to see him in a detention

7

camp. Emil went yesterday. *Walks up to* BAUM: Will the rest take long?

BAUM: Yes. *Counts deliberate turn of crank.* One, two, three. That's the whole run. *Stops.*

ERNST: Good.

BAUM: Oh, I'm a fast worker.

TILLY: Learn it from your father?

BAUM *beginning to clean and pack up machine as* ERNST *takes printed sheets down to table and packs them*: My father? You should have seen him. A dead ringer for Von Hindenburg. A Corporal of 1870. What would happen if he lived today? Some Nazi would say "A war hero," tickle him under the arm—presto! The next day he would be wearing a brown shirt and killing workers a mile a minute. A real smoke.

ERNST: What's the time?

BAUM *looking at watch*: Time for supper. Seven o'clock.

ERNST: Where's Zelda?

TILLY: Said she would be here at six.

ERNST: She is usually on time. Here is the last package to go.

TILLY: I hope Zelda won't crack. She hasn't heard from Hugo for three months.

BAUM *seriously*: Hugo? He might be dead by now. Like the report on Schlagel yesterday. Trying to escape, they said. To fill a man's back full of lead like that. *Puts on a ragged coat.*

ERNST: Take some money for your supper. *Puts coins on table.* This much to spare.

BAUM *shy as a young girl*: I don't like to take it, Ernst.

ERNST: Well, we're even—I don't like to give it. *Indicates machine in box.* Mark it "glass."

BAUM: I used to be crazy on tulip bulbs. For years I spent my weekly salary on them.

TILLY: "Glass" in big letters!

BAUM *doing so*: Do you spell glass with one "s" or two?

ERNST: Two.

TILLY *laughing*: That's one your father didn't teach you.

BAUM: It's no joke. I'm getting dehydrated, that's what I am. Yep, the juices is going right outa me. *Picks up package.* Well, don't take no wooden money. *Exits.*

TILLY: I like him.

ERNST: He's a good worker. *Suddenly shows faintness.*

TILLY *up and to him*: What's the matter, Ernst?

ERNST *sitting*: I guess I'm tired. Maybe the body doesn't throw off disease bugs as easy as I think.

TILLY: If I say you need a month's rest, you'll say "Who does my work?" Is that right?

ERNST: Right!

TILLY: Dammit, I'll do your work.

ERNST: Alone?

TILLY: Why not?

9

ERNST: Tempting, but improbable.

TILLY: You and your male chauvinism!

ERNST *with smiling protest*: No, Tilly, no.

TILLY: Today I'm particularly concerned with you.

ERNST: You want to know a secret? There is something altogether lovely and birdlike about you. *Knock on the door.* Zelda?

TILLY *softly*: I'll see. *She goes, and for a brief moment,* ERNST *allows his real weariness to show, but straightens up as* TILLY *enters with* ZELDA.

ERNST *overbrightly*: Late, Zelda?

ZELDA: Yes, I—I—— *Suddenly begins to cry, head in arms on table.*

ERNST: Dear Zelda, what happened?

TILLY *framing name with lips*: Hugo. ERNST *goes behind* ZELDA *as if to say some comforting thing but realizes better. Looks at* TILLY *and shakes his head pityingly.* ZELDA *finally straightens up and dries her eyes.*

ZELDA: I got the news this morning. They say he jumped out the window. Hugo would do that! They sent the body to his mother. I'll spend the night with her. Is it all right?

ERNST: Sure it is.

ZELDA: I'll deliver the leaflets first. This package? ERNST *nods. She takes it.* Tell the comrades to stay away from the funeral. They'll be watching. ERNST *embraces her, she exits.*

ERNST *in a burst*: Hell! I'd like to go and sit in a park somewhere!

TILLY: They met in the park. She told me once. He was feeding pigeons. You I met on the subway three years ago. Today is an anniversary for us.

ERNST: Really?

TILLY: Zelda took the wind out of my lungs. I wanted to propose....

ERNST: Something nice?

TILLY: A walk in the park—a small supper—then we would walk home slowly, quietly. You'd let me hold your hand.... Poor Zelda.

ERNST: My present dream of the world—I ask for happy laughing people everywhere. I ask for hope in eyes: for wonderful baby boys and girls I ask, growing up strong and prepared for a new world. I won't ever forget the first time we visited the nursery in Moscow. Such faces on those children! Future engineers, doctors; when I saw them I understood most deeply what the revolution meant.

TILLY: Maybe we could have one like that, a baby I mean.

ERNST: When the day comes that we don't have to live like rats in sewers—— Did I thank you for nursing me the past three weeks?

TILLY: Not a word came out of that stingy mouth. *He kisses her in thanks.* Did I thank you for the birthday card?

ERNST: Not a word came out of that stingy mouth. *She kisses him in thanks.* Did I thank you for the woolen socks?

TILLY: Ingratitude! *Kisses her again.* And you Comrade Tausig, I never thanked you just for living!

ERNST: Ahhh . . . *Kisses her fully this time. She finally breaks away.*

TILLY: Stop loafing on my mouth, Comrade. *Looking at papers on table.* We have to finish this.

ERNST: Getting tough again?

TILLY: Seriously, I decoded the milk bill. There are nine names and addresses of party officials to be memorized by your most excellent brain.

ERNST: Berlin?

TILLY: Look it over. The rest of the room's as clean as a plucked chicken. Not a suspicious word.

ERNST: Who's Spitzer? *Examines list.*

TILLY: Rosenfeld, I think.

ERNST: And Strasser?

TILLY: My brother, Hans.

ERNST: Chris' sake, when did you see him last?

TILLY: Four months ago.

ERNST: I think we—— *A low knock on the door stops him. Both freeze into position. From now on they whisper.* Did someone knock?

TILLY *listening*: Just a minute. *Knock is louder.*

ERNST: Don't answer. *Tears name list in half.* Memorize those. Quick!

VOICE *outside*: Open the door!

ERNST: Sisst! *Both stand there memorizing.*

VOICE *as knocking increases*: Open the door—
Secret Police.

TILLY: The Gestapo!

ERNST: That bastard, Zeltner! *Saying address
aloud*: 783-783-783....*Finally the knocking
stops.* Don't stop. *Her lips move rapidly and
silently.* All right?

TILLY: All right. *But she goes on. Knocking
comes again and "Secret Police."* ERNST *lights end
of his paper. Watches her while paper burns.
Finally she nods her head and he touches lighted
paper to hers. Both burn down and are stamped
to dust on the floor.*

ERNST *all in whispers*: You and I were here on
the couch. *Puts coat and vest on back of chair.*

TILLY: An affair?

ERNST: You're in the business. Your room.
Points to himself. Your customer. Push your hair
around. *She does so.*

TILLY: All ready. *Musses up couch.*

VOICE *outside*: Open the door! This is the Secret
Police.

SLOW FADEOUT

In the dark between this scene and the next
the shrill sounds of a half dozen whistles, variously
pitched, slowing with hysterical intensity.

This device to be carried throughout.

SCENE · II

Office in a Nazi brown house. A fat detective in a trench coat and brown derby at telephone on desk which also holds typewriter. His name is POPPER. *Two* ORDERLIES *in Nazi uniform at the side sitting on a bench. They are counting from a list. To one side of the desk stands* ERNST TAUSIG, *a prisoner.*

POPPER *excited and angry on phone*: I'm waiting for you. *Waits, drums fingers, spits.* I'm waiting for you, I said. Mommer God! You think I've got all day.

ORDERLY *begins to count aloud*: Thirty-seven, thirty-eight, thirty-nine——

POPPER *yelling at them*: Dumbbells, can't you see I'm trying to work here. Mommer God, it's full of crazy people, the whole house. Hello! The one I mean is the Communist Ernst Tausig. Find the rest of the report and bring it to me on the third floor immediately. Captain Schlegel is waiting for the report. What? No, Schlegel, S as in Samuel. *Hastily corrects himself.* No, I mean S as in Storm Trooper. Also you made a mistake on the first part of the report. Don't give me back talk, Dumbbell, the report is in front of my eyes here. His girl friend was released. A plain out and out

whore. What? No, not war, whore. *Turns to*
ORDERLY, *in desperation.* You tell him.

ORDERLY 1 *immediately at phone*: W-h-o-r-e.
Retires primly.

POPPER *back at phone*: We brought him in yesterday. So look in the top file right away. *Hangs
up.* Imagine, that nobody tells me it's my fault,
I'll poke my finger through his eye. Such confusion!

ORDERLY 1 *sympathetically*: Terrible!

POPPER: The country is running over with those
red ants. Such confusion.

ORDERLY 2: Terrible!

POPPER: Take the typewriter.

ORDERLY 2: Me?

POPPER: You.

ORDERLY 2: Yes, sir. *Comes over to desk, a
pleasant type.* Where will I take it?

POPPER: What's the matter with you? To type,
to type.

ORDERLY 2: I can't type.

POPPER: You can't type?

ORDERLY 2: No, sir.

POPPER: Dumbbell.

ORDERLY 1: Terrible!

POPPER *to* ORDERLY 1: Can you type?

ORDERLY 1: No, sir.

POPPER: So shut up. Such disorder, such confusion. Every Brown house I was connected with
in the past six months is like this. Mommer God,

they'll say I'm inefficient, they'll kill me. *Suddenly turning on* ERNST: You! You make trouble for Captain Schlegel and I'll—I don't know what I'll do to you. You know where you are?

ERNST: Yes.

POPPER: You know what happens in the Columbia Brown House to Communists?

ERNST: Yes.

POPPER: Why did you say you never lived in Linden Street?

ERNST: I never did.

POPPER *to* ORDERLIES: Did you hear that? He said he never lived there. *To* ERNST: Never in possession of certain illegal materials in connection with the underground work?

ERNST: No.

POPPER *shaking finger under* ERNST'S *nose*: Listen, stinker, I—— *Controls himself, goes back to behind desk.* Write down the liar's answer. *Writes it down himself.* You were last employed by the Musical Instrument Company, Eberhard?

ERNST: Yes.

POPPER: Write down he was last employed by that company. *Writes it down himself. Trooper passes through, whispers, "Courage" to* ERNST. You know we have here enough information to burn you in hell. For three weeks we watched you, you red fox. Do you—— *Suddenly stops as* CAPTAIN SCHLEGEL *enters, followed by an* ORDERLY *named*

ADOLPH. POPPER *continues, fawningly*: Good morning, Captain Schlegel.

SCHLEGEL *a man like Goering*: Is this him?

POPPER: Yes, sir, this is the one, Captain Schlegel.

SCHLEGEL: Any illegal papers found on him?

POPPER: He got rid of them before the arrest, Captain.

SCHLEGEL: Red fighter?

POPPER: Without a doubt, Captain.

SCHLEGEL: Writer?

POPPER: Former editor of a unit paper, Captain.

SCHLEGEL *to* ERNST *as he examines report from desk*: That so?

ERNST: Formerly so.

POPPER: Flat as the rug when you catch them. Otherwise burning Reichstags twice a day.

SCHLEGEL: Never mind. Where's the rest of the report?

POPPER: Begging your pardon, Captain, they can't find it downstairs.

SCHLEGEL: You'd better be careful, Popper. Such inefficiency will not be tolerated.

POPPER *whining*: I do the best I can, Captain.

SCHLEGEL: Never mind, never mind. *To* ERNST: How long have you belonged to the Communist Party?

ERNST: Since 1923.

SCHLEGEL: You deny belonging to the underground party at the present time?

ERNST: I do.

SCHLEGEL: You are on friendly terms with foreigners?

ERNST: No.

SCHLEGEL: You are not familiar with certain Bulgarian incendiaries?

ERNST: No.

SCHLEGEL: Married?

ERNST: No.

SCHLEGEL: Any children?

ERNST *smiling*: No.

SCHLEGEL: What's funny?

ERNST: Nothing.

SCHLEGEL *taking* ERNST *by his coat lapels*: Wipe off the smile. *Releases* ERNST *and dusts off hands as if contaminated.* What unit did you work with?

ERNST: Unit Number twenty-fifteen.

SCHLEGEL: Who was the Unit organizer?

ERNST: A man named Hess.

SCHLEGEL: Where is he now?

ERNST: I saw him last one year ago.

POPPER *until now holding back his eagerness*: Where does he live, huh?

CAPTAIN *gives* POPPER *a superior look.* POPPER *fades apologetically.*

SCHLEGEL: You had charge of a secret printing press on Hartsheim Street?

ERNST: No.

18

SCHLEGEL: You insist you did not help organize the underground press in Berlin.

ERNST: I did not.

SCHLEGEL: No illegal leaflets?

ERNST: No.

SCHLEGEL *goes over and takes rifle from OR-DERLY. Taps twice on floor with butt of rifle, hands it back to* ORDERLY *and returns to* ERNST *at the same time taking the report up from desk:* This report—all a tissue of lies you say?

ERNST: I cannot say.

A MAN *enters—wears mask—limps.*

SCHLEGEL *turning to the man:* What's his name?

MAN: Ernst Taussig.

SCHLEGEL: His work?

MAN: The underground press.

SCHLEGEL: You may go, Zerrago.

MAN *goes.*

ERNST: We knew the rat as Zeltner.

CAPTAIN *suddenly slaps him in the face.*

SCHLEGEL: Control your tongue. When you are asked you will speak, concerning three matters. A, identification of prisoners; B, names; C, addresses. Until then keep quiet. *Turns from him, walks directly away, but suddenly turns and throws the whole sheaf of paper in* ERNST'S *face.*

POPPER: He thinks he's in kindergarten.

SCHLEGEL: You'll be in kindergarten, if you don't keep your face shut. *Approaches* ERNST, *ex-*

amines him from all sides. I hear you're a musician of sorts.

ERNST: Yes.

SCHLEGEL: Play an instrument?

ERNST: Formerly the violin.

SCHLEGEL: Such sensitive hands. Hold them up. ERNST *does so.* So filthy. Put them on the desk. ERNST *does so.* So, a scraper of catgut. Now, what I have against the communists is—*holding and turning* ERNST'S *jaw in his hand*—the snout-like narrowness of their non-Nordic jaws. The nostrils display sensual and voluptuous self-indulgence, talking with the aid of hands and feet; non-Nordic characteristics. *Walking away from* ERNST, *wipes his hands on a handkerchief.*

ADOLPH: For every S. A. man killed in Berlin, Brandenburg, three communists will have to answer with their lives.

SCHLEGEL: A violin is an eloquent instrument. Perhaps you are familiar with Beethoven's Opus sixty-one, the violin concerto. Answer yes or no.

ERNST: Yes.

SCHLEGEL: In the key of D? *Having taken rifle from* ORDERLY'S *hand, he suddenly brings down the butt of it on* ERNST'S *fingers, smashing them. Roars:* With the JOACHIM CADENZA? ERNST, *writhing with pain, puts his smashed right hand under his left armpit and almost faints.* CAPTAIN SCHLEGEL *now roars the rest:* And if you think that's the end, let me tell you by tomorrow you'll find your neck half broken instead of three lousy fingers!!! Stand up straight! Do you hear me? ERNST *straightens up*. Put your hand down. Put it down!!! ERNST *slowly does so*. In ten minutes your old slut of a mother won't know you. *Suddenly, softly:* Unless you answer my questions. *Waits.* You refuse...?

ERNST *finally, controlling his pain:* I have nothing to say.

SCHLEGEL: Take him to the barrack rooms. Take him out of my sight.

ORDERELY 2: Yes, sir.

SCHLEGEL *to* ORDERLY 1: Get out.

ORDERLY 1: Yes, sir. *Exits quickly.*

SCHLEGEL: We've been too easy with that one.

POPPER: Yes, sir, he's a fresh guy.

SCHLEGEL: What the hell are they saving him for?

POPPER: I can't say. I seen the order myself signed by Major Duhring. Handle him with kid gloves, it says. He was in a position to know a big pile of names and addresses. Major Duhring is expected next week to personally question him.

SCHLEGEL *bitterly:* Duhring? Duhring?

POPPER: He's soft as butter but he knows how to make them talk.

SCHLEGEL: Oh, I see he can make them talk, but I can't.

POPPER: No, Captain, I only meant——

SCHLEGEL: Get out. You make me vomit.

21

POPPER: Yes, Captain. *Bows his way out backwards and bunks into chair. Exits.*

SCHLEGEL *turning around the room in anger*: I think that Popper one must have Jewish blood. He hasn't the brains of a trained flea. What strikes you as being funny, Adolph?

ADOLPH: How that fat slob bowed his way out.

SCHLEGEL: I have seen you in a few peculiar positions at times. In fact, it might be much better for both of us if you weren't so graceful with those expressive hands of yours. Flitting around here like a soulful antelope. I'm lonely, I've got no one in the whole world.

ADOLPH: You've got me, Eric.

SCHLEGEL: Hitler is lonely too. So is God.

ADOLPH: I know.

SCHLEGEL: I lost my temper and smashed him against orders.

ADOLPH: You need a rest. You're nervous.

SCHLEGEL: Say it—nervous as a woman—say it! Yes, that's the third one in a week I haven't been able to get a word out of. All I need is for them to find out about us and I am through for good. My God, you don't know who to trust.

ADOLPH: Trust me.

SCHLEGEL *examining* ADOLPH's *face between his hands*. You? You're as fickle as a girl. You know that song by Hugo Wolf, I wish all your charm was painted. It's written for you and me. Last night I heard a lieder concert. There weren't fifty people in the audience. The country is gripped by fear. Houses are locked by day and night.

ADOLPH: Please . . . I'm very fond of you.

SCHLEGEL: Fond? You probably carry tales. . . . I know, you love the Captain's uniform, not the man.

ADOLPH: You're hurting me.

SCHLEGEL: What does a child like you know?

ADOLPH: Please, I mean. . . . *Suddenly begins to cry.*

SCHLEGEL: Sisst! You'll drive me crazy. Where do you think you are? Go out and wash your face. *Looks at papers on desk.* Who's crazy, they or me? Saving a communist because they think he'll spill the beans. I thought I told you to go.

ADOLPH: Please.

SCHLEGEL: Get out of here, don't you hear me? Get out!

ADOLPH: Yes, sir. *Hurries out.*

SCHLEGEL *looks at papers, scatters them around*: My God! My God! What's the world coming to? Where's it going? My God!

BLACKOUT

Whistles in the dark

SCENE · III

The barracks room. TROOPERS *playing pinochle. Drink beer. Guns and blackjacks on table.* FIVE PRISONERS *lined up against wall, backs to audience.* YOUNG TROOPER *marching back and forth behind them.* PELTZ *and* WEINER, *two troopers, having a hot argument downstage.*

PELTZ: I'm always for the practical side of the thing.

WEINER: Was you ever in a school, if I'm not getting too personal?

PELTZ: I went to school.

WEINER: Where, if I'm not getting too personal?

PELTZ: Right here in Berlin. We learned all that stuff in school, Napoleon an' all that stuff, but it didn't help in business. Adages an' all that. They're for the idlers. When I was in business we didn't talk about Napoleon. We talked about how much.

WEINER: You are absolutely without doubt the most ignorant man I ever met.

PELTZ: I know, I know, we just don't agree.

WEINER: What made Von Hindenburg a great general?

24

PELTZ: There was other great generals besides him.

WEINER: There never was a greater one.

PELTZ: How about the few others who was great? Don't you know every generation must have its magnet? You don' see that!

WEINER: What's the use of arguing. It's like religion. Some say——

PELTZ: You got that student stuff, artistic. Me, I'm more for the practical side. But you are a good scholar. Yes, I can see that, Weiner. Was you always that way? More on the student side.

WEINER: What? What the hell are you talking about?

PELTZ: Now you know——

WEINER: You're so dumb! *Walks away.* PELTZ *shrugs his shoulders, goes back to newspaper.*

YOUNG TROOPER *to Elderly Man:* Can't you stand still when you're told to stand still!! *Kicks him strongly;* MAN *falls; trooper picks him up.* You weren't too old to be a Social-Democrat, were you!! *Shoves him back in line.* ANOTHER *brings in* TWO MORE PRISONERS—*One feebly attempts a Nazi salute, says,* "Heil Hitler," *but is shoved in line.*

TROOPER 1 *at table:* The bastards think they'll save their skin like that!

TROOPER 2 *squirts beer from mouth at prisoner.*

YOUNG TROOPER: The old one wanted a good day's rest on the floor.

TROOPER 2: Which one? *Goes to him with bottle.*

YOUNG TROOPER: This one. TROOPER 2 *fills mouth with beer, squirts it in* OLD MAN's *face.* ALL *roar with laughter.*

TROOPER 1 *coming over:* Dammit! I know this one. You know where you are?

BOY: Yes sir.

TROOPER 1 *points to boy:* You was here before, wasn't you?

BOY: Yes sir.

TROOPER 1: What was you arrested for that time?

BOY: I was accused of distributing pamphlets.

TROOPER 1: And what now?

TROOPER 5: Riding on a truck load of illegal literature.

TROOPER 1: Jesus, Mary and Joseph!

BOY: He came up to me—the man. I was standing on the corner and he offered me five marks to help drive the load.

TROOPER 2: You didn't know what was in the boxes?

BOY: No, he didn't tell me that and I didn't ask questions.

TROOPER 1: This little one is telling fairy tales.

BOY: I was glad to earn the five marks.

TROOPER 3 *at the table:* What did you do it for? They won't believe you now.

BOY: I didn't work since I left school. The

26

labor camps won't accept me because I'm a Communist. What can I do?

TROOPER 1: What you can do? Eat floor wax! *Hits him; the* BOY *falls.* Good appetite!

TROOPER 3 *coming forward:* Leave the boy alone, Max!

TROOPER 5: Look at these remarks. *Reads from pamphlets.* "The Brutal Slaughter of Red Front Comrades by Hitler's Brown Murder-Hordes——"

TROOPER 1: Jesus, Mary and Joseph! *Kicks the fallen boy.*

TROOPER 3: Leave the boy alone, Max. *Sorry for him.*

TROOPER 1: I'll leave him alone!

TROOPER 4 *still at the table with handful of cards:* If you're playing cards, play.

TROOPER 3: Play cards, Max!

TROOPER 1: All right, Professor. *The game begins and presently* POPPER *walks in with* ERNST.

POPPER: Over there. ERNST *goes into line.* POPPER *watches fallen* BOY *get up into line.* What happened with him?

TROOPER 3: The thunderbolt made a visit. *Indicates* TROOPER 1.

TROOPER 1 *jumping up:* You are just too damn smart, Hassel!

POPPER: Silence! POPPER *goes to them, whispers.* THEY *nod heads as they furtively look* ERNST *over.* POPPER *says, "Don't forget" and exits.* TROOPER 2 *marches around* OTTO *and examines him insolently. Goes back to seat and says to others:*

TROOPER 2: Not a blemish on the lily!

TROOPER 4: Are we playing cards or not?

TROOPER 1: I will say three fifty in spades.

TROOPER 2: You pay double if you lose.

TROOPER 1: Don't put no evil eye on me, Hassel!

TROOPER 2: Don't you act so mean, Herr Thunderbolt!

TROOPER 1: You wanna make something of it?

TROOPER 2: To me you can't talk like to your snotnose friends!

TROOPER 1: You must think——

TROOPER 3: Boys! Is this the trust the Leader puts in you—to start fights in the barracks with Jews and Bolsheviks watching you.

TROOPER 2: That's right!

TROOPER 4: Heil Hitler. ALL *salute as if toasting and all sit. Card improvisation.* TROOPER *scene.* WEINER *edges his way over to* PELTZ.

WEINER: What kind of education can you get from the newspapers?

PELTZ: I see how it is. You like to lay around in those cafés with all the Bohemians. See them lying around with frocks on—dreamers. They can't come to the front—just dreamers.

WEINER: Did you read what Thyssen said?

PELTZ: A big man, a big man.

WEINER: Success is ninety per cent luck, five per cent work, he said.

28

PELTZ: Exactly, exactly, an' don't any intelligent man say the same? The same thing, he says, the same.

WEINER: What?

PELTZ: That means something, don't it? *Improvisation on pinochle game goes on in loud voices. The* OLD MAN *who has been swaying now falls again. The* YOUNG TROOPER *looking over a shoulder at the game finally turns and sees the fallen man.*

YOUNG TROOPER: Look at him—can't stand no more. *Examines him.* He's bleeding from the mouth.

TROOPER 3: Take him to the hospital. My trick.

TROOPER 1: He's been standing seven hours.

OLD MAN: Don't hit me, please don't hit me.

YOUNG TROOPER: No, just dusting you off. *Hits hard.*

OLD MAN: Please don't hit me. I was in the war. I was decorated for bravery. Von Macksen decorated me for merit.

YOUNG TROOPER: *General* Von Macksen.

OLD MAN: I swear. Don't hit me again. I swear I—Yes, I was—*Now laughs and goes very hysterical.* . . . Please, please. . . . *The* THUNDERBOLT *runs over—hits the* OLD MAN *who crumples silently.*

TROOPER 1: These Social Democrats is a noisy bunch. *Has retained hand of cards. Starts back to table and on way says: "The ace of diamonds,"* puts *it on table, says to* YOUNG TROOPER: Court-plaster on his head, Fritz! *The* YOUNG TROOPER *drags the* OLD MAN *out like a sack of sawdust.*

TROOPER 4 *as they play cards:* Your muscle's better than his.

TROOPER 1: Whose?

TROOPER 4: Tauchner in 120. He bets anything he can knock a man out in one blow—nine out of ten. Why, yesterday he won fifteen marks and a smoking pipe.

TROOPER 2: That's scientific. Just how you hit them . . . like tearing telephone books.

TROOPER 1: I guess you can do it too!

TROOPER 2: If I want . . .

TROOPER 1: Only you don't want?

TROOPER 2: Maybe I'll show you and maybe I won't.

TROOPER 1: How about a bet—the pack of cards against my belt?

TROOPER 2: With the silver buckle? *A scream heard from below.*

TROOPER 1: Yeah.

TROOPER 2: You go first.

TROOPER 1: Then you go and if I don't do it, you go again.

TROOPER 2: That's right.

TROOPER 4: Hand over the bets. *They do so.* Try the one Popper brought in. He's the biggest and freshest. *Calls to* ERNST. Hey Blackhead! Fall out of line! *Pulls him out by coat tail.* Stand there, pig. ERNST *stands in place.* TROOPER 3 *stays at table. The* OTHERS *approach.*

TROOPER 2: Who takes this one?

TROOPER 1: You're his size. I'll take that boy. Hey—! *Pulls out* BOY.

TROOPER 4: I count three. You both hit together. Ready.

TROOPER 2 *preparing for blow with the other:* Yes, ready . . .

TROOPER 4: Gentlemen, one . . . TROOPER 1 *spits on his fist.* TROOPER 2 *stands motionless. The* BOY *at the count of two will cover his face with his hands.*

TROOPER 2: Remember, only in the head!

TROOPER 4: Gentlemen—two!

BOY *covering face:* No.

TROOPER 1: Put your hands down, stinker! BOY *refuses.* Put them down, bastard!! BOY *does so.*

TROOPER 4: Gentlemen—two and a half. . . .

TROOPER 2: Just a minute.

TROOPER 1: What's the matter——

TROOPER 2: Yours is half fainting—a push-over——

TROOPER 1: Well, I'll take him. You! *Pulls another out—pushes* BOY *who falls sitting and cries monotonously.*

TROOPER 4: Now—1—2—3——! BOTH MEN *let blows fly. The victim of No. 1 goes down in a heap.* ERNST *stands stunned. In disgust* TROOPER 2 *goes back to seat.*

TROOPER 1 *delighted:* Well, who is the big scientist now?

TROOPER 2: That was a pushover.

TROOPER 4: Max won the bet. *Hands over the prizes to* TROOPER 1.

TROOPER 1: You wasn't so smart. *Suddenly* TROOPER 2 *in a fury lets fly at* ERNST *who slowly crumples to his knees.*

TROOPER 2: Get back in the line, you louse! *Stalks back to table and sits moodily with chin on fist.* ERNST *slowly crawls back into line and rises painfully.*

TROOPER 3: Fritzie, get a bucket of water for the kid. *He laughs triumphantly.*

TROOPER 1: Ha, ha, Professor! *Laughs.* Trooper scene. PELTZ *and* WEINER *have been arguing throughout this last scene.*

PELTZ: Oh, there's no question, no question. Then what's the use of cursing the world and blaming it on a handful of rich men?

WEINER *disgusted completely:* I'm not cursing the world!

PELTZ: Now you was pretty strong there. Tell the truth, wasn't you, Weiner?

WEINER: All I said was——

PELTZ: I don't care what this one or that one says about the rich men. It really don't interest me. Or taxes or socialism. I don't listen to them artists. But just because there's a depression I wouldn't say, "Oh, the goddamn rich men."

WEINER: I didn't say the goddamn rich men.

PELTZ: Absolutely, absolutely . . .

WEINER: My God, you're dumb! If I'm not getting too personal.

PELTZ: I know, Weiner, I know. Naturally people ain't of the same temper-a-ment. Naturally . . . the practical side—like Herr Doctor Goebbels says here in the paper. *Reads.* "The head of of a prominent Jew must be displayed on every telegraph pole from Munich to Berlin." No dreamy stuff, Weiner. That's practical. . . . *A scream heard from below.*

FADEOUT

33

SCENE · IV

*The same as 3. Nazi swastika flag
as background.* ORDERLIES 1 *and* 2
rediscovered, respectively EDSEL
and MARTIN.

EDSEL: "What's the world comin' to," he says to
poppa. Poppa began cryin'. My uncle said, "Don't
cry 'cause it won't help nothin'." After all he didn't
work for three years.

MARTIN: The leader has promised a job to every
German.

EDSEL: Don't you think I said that? "Read the
papers," I told him. "Plenty of work in Munich."
So he laughs and says that he just came from
Munich and not a job to be had there. But their
papers say plenty of jobs in Berlin.

MARTIN: That sounds to me like red propaganda.
Why didn't you arrest him?

EDSEL: My own uncle?

MARTIN: He told a lie, didn't he?

EDSEL: I don't know.

MARTIN: The Leader says there's jobs for every-
one.

EDSEL: I know. . . .

MARTIN: Government work on the roads.

EDSEL: Two and a half marks a week. Can a
mouse live on it?

MARTIN: Is that a nice thing to say?

34

EDSEL: Well, can a mouse live on it?

MARTIN: I don't know. Dr. Goebbels spoke on the radio last night. He says we must be prepared for a war with them any day.

EDSEL: Momma said some Jews was very nice people.

MARTIN *jumps up and goes away:* Say, you better be careful—saying things like that. I don't wanna even know you.

EDSEL: Oh, she says it. Of course I don't agree.

MARTIN: You better be careful. They're hot as hornets around here today. This morning they found the zoölogical garden plastered with red propaganda. They can't find out who done it. They cleaned them all away on one side and when they turned around it was all plastered up on the other side.

EDSEL: They will lose their heads, all them Communists.

MARTIN: Of course. . . .

EDSEL: If they catch them.

MARTIN: The Major brought in some of the leaflets for examination. Right there on the desk.

EDSEL *backs away from desk as if stung.*

EDSEL: Those things there?

MARTIN: The tissue paper—they print it on tissue papers so the wind blows them all over. A certain lady on Friedrichstrasse, one flew right on her face and when she seen what it was she fainted dead away.

35

EDSEL *craning his neck for a look at the desk:* Can you see what they say? Read what it says.

MARTIN: Say, read it yourself.

EDSEL: You're closer to the desk than me.

MARTIN *they are whispering now:* It don't prove nothing 'cause I'm closer to the desk. *Slowly edges over. Looks around. Finally whispers:* "Workers of Germany!" *Springs away, amazed at his own audacity.*

EDSEL *whispering:* What?

MARTIN: That's what it says. . . .

EDSEL *both whispering:* Read some more, Martin, Shh. *Tiptoes to right side and watches out.*

MARTIN *looks around and tiptoes to desk. Picks up slip nervously, clears throat, reads:* "The Krupp armament works ran at a loss until Hitler came into power. Now it announces a 6% dividend ——" *Breaks off nervously.* Watch out, Edsel.

EDSEL: I'm watching. *Looks off left.*

MARTIN *looks left, continues nervously, in a whisper:* "While five and a half million workers are unemployed, which, with their families, constitutes one-third of the German working class, increased military forces are the basis of the Hitler economic..." *Paper drops out of his nervous hands.*

EDSEL: Pick it up.

MARTIN: I can't.

EDSEL *comes over:* What are you so nervous for?

MARTIN *chattering:* Who's nervous?

EDSEL *himself shaking:* You're sweating.

MARTIN: It's a hot day.

EDSEL: Stand at the door. MARTIN *does so.* EDSEL *looks around, then picks up paper; reads:* "In the meantime there is no bread, no milk. The Hitler-controlled newspapers print lies. The——"

MARTIN *suddenly panic-struck:* The Major! EDSEL *runs around not knowing where to put the slip. Tries to find a place. Suddenly puts it in his mouth and chews violently. As* MAJOR DUHRING *enters, ceases chewing and with* MARTIN *comes rigidly to attention.* MAJOR *walks in, notices* EDSEL.

MAJOR: What's wrong?

MARTIN: Beg pardon, sir?

MAJOR *pointing to* EDSEL *who has a mouthful:* You! *Waits.* Can't talk? EDSEL *finally swallows strongly.*

EDSEL: Yes, sir?

MAJOR: Why are you men loafing around here?

EDSEL: Beg pardon, sir, we were assigned to this room.

MAJOR: What room?

EDSEL: To the examination room.

MAJOR: Now boys, does this look like an examination room? Clear out before I lose my temper. *They scramble out with heels clicking and salutes.* All right, all right, get out. *Laughs when they exit, a tired civilized man. Calls one back.* You!

MARTIN *badly scared:* Yes, sir, this is not the examination room.

MAJOR: Here, don't stand there like a whipped dog. I'm not calling you down. Inform them on the floor below to send up the Communist, Ernst Tausig.

BOTH *bowing and scraping:* Yes, sir. *Try to get out of door together and comic mixup, finally out.*

MAJOR *shakes head with pity:* Hmmm. . . . *Picks up red leaflet.* "Workers of Germany. . . ." *Puts down slip, shakes his head again. Goes up to Nazi insignia, examines it reflectively, with bitterness.* ERNST *is brought in. His back still turned, says to* ORDERLY: Leave us alone. ORDERLY *clicks heels, salutes.* MAJOR *with back turned:* Sit down, Tausig. ERNST, *wearied, mistrustful, does not move.* MAJOR *slowly turns, handkerchief at lower portion of face.*

MAJOR: What? Another whipped and frightened dog? You may be seated. . . . ERNST *looks at him a long time and finally sits.* Cigarette? . . . ERNST *takes one,* MAJOR *putting it in his mouth and lighting it. Waits to see what* MAJOR *has up his sleeve.* You look different, Tausig, than when I saw you last—a meeting—in Charlottenburg.

ERNST: I remember you—Duhring.

MAJOR: What happened to your hand?

ERNST: What happened to your "social ideals?"

MAJOR: Why I am in a Nazi uniform happens to be unimportant. A realistic necessity. I am married into one of the finest old German families, Nordic from the year one. The work I do for the National Socialists harms no foe of the Nazi state; in fact I am inclined to believe that if the truth were known, my work may often be interpreted as a positive hindrance. *Laughs, and then adds soberly.* Not for publication. Perhaps I don't care. ... That's nearer the truth. I will not deny the justness of the scorn in your eyes. This may cost me my head. ... I'm not sure I care. *Turns around room and comes back.* I want to warn you.... They'll get what they want out of you. Trust me to——

ERNST *bitterly:* A man tortured by his conscience?

MAJOR: Call it what you will. Here they use—— *Voices heard without.* MAJOR *harshly, tearing cigarette from* ERNST's *mouth.* Stand up! When these three questions are answered—— *Breaks off to greet a blonde* WOMAN *escorted by* CAPTAIN SCHLEGEL. Good afternoon, dear.

HEDVIG *his wife, vacuous but energetic:* Ruppert, the handsome captain showed me the way. I had to ask your advice about an important matter.

MAJOR *ironically to* CAPTAIN: Thank you, Captain.

SCHLEGEL *with ironic courtesy himself:* You're welcome, Major. Your wife and I chatted pleasantly for ten minutes on the lower floor before I realized her identity.

HEDVIG: Yes, the place is full of nasty-mannered men. They kept me waiting ten minutes. *Suddenly aware of* ERNST. Who is this?

MAJOR *with ironic intent*: A Communist, Hedvig. . . .

HEDVIG *shrinking away to other side of desk, now protected by* CAPTAIN: Oh!

MAJOR *smiling in spite of himself*: They don't bite.

SCHLEGEL. Only in the dark.

HEDVIG: Such dirty beasts. Don't they ever wash?

MAJOR: When they have the facilities.

HEDVIG: And these were the ones who were supposed to be masters of the coming new world. *Slaps him with glove.* ERNST *stands unflinchingly. She drops her glove.* CAPTAIN *picks it up and proffers it to her.* Oh, no, I couldn't wear it again. CAPTAIN *puts it on desk.* MAJOR *takes it up.*

MAJOR *ironic*: They're expensive gloves. What was on your mind, Hedvig?

HEDVIG: About my broadcast speech. *Takes it from purse.*

MAJOR: Did you write it yourself, Hedvig?

HEDVIG: No, Poppa's secretary wrote it, but of course I believe every word of it myself, so it's the same thing, isn't it?

MAJOR: I should think so, Hedvig. *With ironic seriousness.*

HEDVIG: I wanted you to hear it before I broadcasted. I don't have to tell you that at least a half million German housewives——

MAJOR: Will put down their housework to listen to Hedvig von Barbossa explain their reason for existence.

HEDVIG: Oh, you! Always anticipating my next word!

MAJOR: A perfect husband. Don't you think so, Captain Schlegel?

CAPTAIN *ironic. A constant fight goes on between the two men:* By all means.

MAJOR: Hedvig, we are having a very heavy day here.

SCHLEGEL *ironic:* Oh, very heavy. MAJOR *gives him a penetrating look—a slight duel goes on between their eyes.*

MAJOR: So I must ask you to merely give me the gist of the speech, dear. Suppose we say, merely the summation.

HEDVIG: Oh you! You just aren't interested in my intellectual development.

SCHLEGEL *ironic:* Your husband is really the busiest officer in our section.

MAJOR: That answers you, my dear. So merely the gist.

HEDVIG: Well . . . I thought I would conclude as follows. *Reads speech:* "Women must understand their part in this moral renaissance of the German people. Well has it been said by our great leader, 'In eternal warfare mankind will become great. In eternal peace mankind would be ruined.' Yes, my dear friends, war alone puts the stamp of greatness on a people! Let women tend the home! Let women breed warriors! Let women forget the pursuit of culture! Germany must expand! Germany must push her frontiers east and west! Women of Germany, give your lives for this cause!" Is that all right, Ruppert?

MAJOR: Splendid—The whole theory of the fascist state in a paragraph. You might be one of our leading theoreticians one of these days.

HEDVIG: I told Poppa's secretary what to write, I truly did.

MAJOR: Yes, now you must run along, Hedvig. Leave us to our work. Good-by.

HEDVIG: And remember dinner at the Hauptmann's tonight.

MAJOR: I won't forget. Captain, please see my wife safely out.

SCHLEGEL: Yes, sir. *Goes with her.*

MAJOR *to* ERNST: You see the sort of convenient marriages one can sometimes be forced to make.

ERNST: The captain is not your friend.

MAJOR: Nor yours. *Indicating wife's glove in his hand:* The captain suspects me of leniency to prisoners. My lineage. *In a sudden emotional outburst:* I tell you a civilized human can't stand it! A great sermon requiem is being played. It's a nightmare! *Gets himself in control.* He holds his knowledge over my head like a sword—the captain, I mean. In turn I have collected certain data concerning the captain's private life and loves—enough to have him purged to a blood stain on the wall! We will duel ourselves to death, we two! This amuses you?

ERNST: Yes.

MAJOR: I can understand. Briefly, here is some information. *Business-like, now.* You can take it or leave it, Tausig. Our side wants information from you. Addresses and names of party officials.

ERNST: Don't have them!

MAJOR: I'm not asking. They're sure you can identify prisoners. They mean to make you do it. You've been here three weeks. Until now they've been comparatively mild. They'll beat you to within an inch of death. You won't want to live. Then they'll nurse you back to health. This will happen several times.

ERNST: I will remember my proletarian task.

MAJOR: It's possible you may forget your proletarian task. Don't smile. A man's made of flesh and bone. They'll inform your comrades through subversive means that you've turned stool pigeon. Before you know it your own unit papers will be passing the word along. In a few months—no friends. No home. Only the new clothes and money in the pocket this side will furnish to keep up the fraud. You still smile? But suppose they put you next to the driver when they make raids? Suppose you are stood outside the courtroom where your

43

comrades will be tried for treason? Will they understand the truth of your position? That's right—screw up your face. . . .

ERNST: My hand hurts.

MAJOR: Get medical attention on the way out. I'll sign an order.

ERNST: On the way out?

MAJOR: On the way out! That's the first step. We're releasing you. You're expected to make contacts with other party members. You'll be followed every minute of the day and night. If you don't prove valuable—*hands over signed medical order*—back you come . . . and then begins the breaking-down process. *Stops.* Listen, take my advice. There is an easier way out. . . .

ERNST: What is that?

MAJOR: Shoot yourself. There is peace and quiet in the grave. *Quotes:* "So I returned and considered all the oppressions that are done under the sun . . . wherefore I praised the dead." SCHLEGEL *enters.*

MAJOR: Very good.

SCHLEGEL: The compliments of General Goering and staff, who will pay us a visit this afternoon.

MAJOR *wary:* Very good. You saw my wife safely to the door?

SCHLEGEL: To her car.

MAJOR: Very good.

SCHLEGEL: Our prisoner displays a most fraternal attitude. *Nods towards seated* ERNST.

MAJOR: Judging from the success of the prisoner's political party in distributing illegal literature, it might be well to fraternize with them in order to learn the secrets of that success.

SCHLEGEL: I resent such remarks before a prisoner. Stand up, you! ERNST *stands.*

MAJOR: With both of us in one room I give orders. Remain seated. ERNST *sits.*

SCHLEGEL: Major, I regret to inform you as house captain that it is my duty to make various reports concerning——

MAJOR: Silence! *Furious.*

SCHLEGEL: Aside from your shoulder straps I am——

MAJOR: Goddamit! Silence!

SCHLEGEL *turns and walks to door, white with inner rage. Stops, turns:* Jew!

MAJOR: What?

SCHLEGEL: You didn't think I knew that?

MAJOR: Come here. *Other slowly approaches.*

SCHLEGEL *coolly:* What's on your mind? *They look at each other eye to eye.*

MAJOR *finally:* What do you mean?

SCHLEGEL: Does your wife know that?

MAJOR: Know what?

SCHLEGEL: Obviously staff headquarters has never made a close examination of the Duhring family tree.

MAJOR: If I hear one more word out of your mouth—— *Catches and twists his tunic.*

SCHLEGEL: You'll do that?

MAJOR: With my own hands.

SCHLEGEL *with smiling insolence*: By gun or sword? Here is one of 38 caliber. *Insolently hands over gun from his own holster*. The first instinct of the Jew is to run.

At this close range the MAJOR *suddenly pulls the gun trigger. The* CAPTAIN *gets the whole automatic charge in the belly. Grabs himself with both hands. Slowly crumples in a soft pile. Gets to desk—falls behind it*. MAJOR *finally speaks in a soft voice*.

MAJOR: I didn't want to do it. He asked for it—— ADOLPH *runs in*. Wait outside. You will escort this prisoner to the street when he leaves the room.

ADOLPH *seeing body*: Very good. *Exits smartly*.

ERNST *finally*: You're in trouble.

MAJOR: It need not concern you. *Eyes still on body*. One thing: see your girl if you like. She reported as a prostitute, not a party worker—which she is.

ERNST: You're mistaken.

MAJOR: I'm telling you! Not asking! See her— it's all right, she won't be molested. And for God's sake give some good girl a kiss for me. I am so slimed over with rottenness.... "Red Front" I can't say to you.... But "United Front"—I say that. In every capitalist country in the world this day let them work for the united front.

46

ERNST: I know.

MAJOR: Have the hand fixed. You have the pass. Good luck.... Just a second—cigarettes—— *Gives pack.* Say I am not despised. Please say it.

ERNST: No—really, you are not despised.

MAJOR: You are talking to a dying man.

ERNST: With so much work to do?

MAJOR: I did the work—like an embezzling bank teller—I destroyed three files of valuables information against your comrades this morning. With this murder on my hands, what is to be expected. You see, the contradictions of my own nature have backed up on me. Get out!

ERNST: Thanks. *He slowly goes.* MAJOR *stands there. Looks at dead body. Goes back to desk. Sits jauntily on it. Whistles a snatch. Examines and twirls his own gun, thinks about and touches various vulnerable spots of his physiognomy, finally concentrates on one spot, places handkerchief over gun hand—stops. Suddenly puts gun on desk, looks at uniform, removes coat or Nazi arm band. Tears flag off wall.... Picks up gun—puts muzzle in mouth.*

Simultaneously with BLACKOUT there is a shot fired. Whistles in the dark.

SCENE · V

In the dark, under the whistles we pick up on radio music, full and classical. With the lights fading up we see TILLY'S *small room. A rough cot. One window looking out on a world of clear light. A small bureau, wash basin and pitcher of water on it. A door.* TILLY *in an old bathrobe. Music coming from her little radio.* TILLY *dips a corner of a towel in the water, slowly wipes her face clean with it. She finishes. Turns down cot covers. Goes to window, raises shade— Blue night light comes in. She turns down lamp. Turns off radio, but puts it on again. Sits on bed and just as she bends to remove slippers there is a tap on her door. She stays in her bent position for a second, finally when a second knock comes—she slithers to the door. Listens. The knock again.*

TILLY *in a faint whisper:* Who is it?
VOICE: Ernst....

TILLY *does not believe it. Comes to center of room. Listens, looks around, finally in a full impulse goes to door. Throws it open.* ERNST *is there.*

48

*She is away from door. He slowly comes in, closes
door, stands against it. For a long time they look
at each other silently, finally:* Ernst!

ERNST *and they are in each other's arms:* Tilly!

TILLY: Alive!

ERNST: Alive!

TILLY: Please, sit here on the bed. *She escorts him
to the bed. He sits. She lowers shade. Turns on
lamp. Turns and looks at him; is shocked by his
appearance.* Dear.... *She throws herself at his feet,
on her knees, holds him as a mother might do with
a child.* You're hurt....

ERNST: Not as much as I might be. Only my
back is raw ... the shirt is stuck to it.

TILLY: Here, I'll fix it. *Goes to wet towel.*

ERNST: No, darling, if you touch me there I'll
faint.

TILLY: Are you hungry?

ERNST: No, dear, no. Here, someone gave me
cigarettes. We'll smoke and talk. Don't be excited.
I want news. Here—— *They light cigarettes. She
gets a little ashtray—they sit together on cot.*

TILLY: News, what news? You've been released.

ERNST: They held me in the Columbia House
since the arrest. I counted the days when I could
remember—twenty-two....

TILLY: Twenty-three, Ernst.

ERNST: You counted too.

TILLY: What then?

ERNST: You don't know what happens, you

don't know. No one knows until he walks through that hell. . . .

TILLY: Why have they released you?

ERNST: I am being followed. I'm expected to make party contacts. Don't look out the window. Two of them in the grocery doorway. . . . I couldn't give them the slip. Maybe I shouldn't have come.

TILLY: A man must have some place.

ERNST: It won't harm. We fooled them about your identity. Where's Carl?

TILLY: Safe at work in the suburbs.

ERNST: Good.

TILLY: Were you afraid there?

ERNST: A man who knows that the world contains millions of brothers and sisters can't be afraid. Don't think I haven't screamed with pain—they have ways of arousing every corpuscle to pain—but you keep your mouth shut.

TILLY: Your hand. . . .

ERNST *wincing*: Don't touch it. *Gets up. Walks away.*

TILLY: Sit down again. Don't be afraid of softness, of sorrow. . . .

ERNST *holds back his emotional impulse to cry on her shoulder. Finally*: What news of the others?

TILLY: Raff is dead.

ERNST *deeply touched*: How?

TILLY: The report they gave out was that he jumped from a window. And Hans Mathieson. . . .

ERNST: The same?

TILLY: The same.

ERNST: Those brave fighters....

TILLY: I'm glad you're living, Ernst.

ERNST *suddenly crying out in protest*: Tilly, I must tell you. Tilly, for a week I have been chewing my heart to pieces. All the time I was in the Brown House they were offering me bribes, any inducements to turn informer. First a session of endearment. Then a session of torture. The human body is a tower of strength. After a while comes numbness, but the mind begins to wander. I'm afraid, Tilly—do you hear that, afraid! Something might happen. There is no rest, no possible contact with party members permitted. They will seize me again, return me to the same program. I'm afraid of what might happen. I ask for one hour of peace.

TILLY: Peace in this war?

ERNST: Yes, peace! In the cell there—I know I stayed alive because I knew my comrades were with me in the same pain and chaos. Yes, I know that till the day I die there is no peace for an honest worker in the whole world.

TILLY: Till the day we die there is steady work to do. Let us hope we will both live to see strange and wonderful things. Perhaps we will die before then. Our children will see it then. Ours!

ERNST *bitterly*: Our children!

TILLY: I'm going to have a baby, Ernst....

ERNST: Who is?

TILLY: I am.

ERNST: You mean it?

TILLY: Your baby. *Dawn—where even the tea-kettle sings from happiness.*

ERNST *finally, after looking at her and not knowing what to say:* Please, allow me to change the subject.... Overgaard, I met him three streets away from here. I made signals with my eyes. He understood. Passed by like a stranger. *Finally:* A baby?

TILLY: Yes.

ERNST *walks to window:* It's almost morning....

TILLY *joining him:* Ernst, the tenderness I feel for you.... I don't know how to say.... Part of my deepest life came back to me when you walked in the door here. You keep coming up in my eyes like the sense of tears....

ERNST: I understand.

TILLY: It is true our work comes before our personal happiness. But we must try to wrest some joy from life.

ERNST: How can that be when presently I shall be a decoy to trap other wild ducks?

TILLY: We'll manage. Escape is possible one way or another. Now I want you to undress and sleep.

ERNST: Sleep?

TILLY: Under the warm blankets.

ERNST: Sleep in your little bed? My sister, comrade ... my wife.... *Sits on bed. She takes off his shoes. His coat. He winches as he stretches out.*

TILLY: It hurts?

ERNST: Yes.

TILLY: Tomorrow we'll fix all these things. Sleep, Ernst, sleep. Tomorrow you can read the full report on the united front. *L'Humanité* came through, several copies.

ERNST *suddenly sitting up:* What united front?

TILLY: The united front in France.

ERNST: It has happened?

TILLY: I thought you knew?

ERNST: In France they have joined to make a solid front against the fascists?

TILLY: Please don't get so excited, Ernst. *Tries to calm him.*

ERNST: Our work is bearing fruit? In that beautiful classic country. The united front? Oh Tilly, oh Tilly!! *And suddenly he is crying in the pillow for all his pains and for the joy of this news.* TILLY *soothes him with understanding.*

TILLY: Yes, cry, cry.... *She strokes him until the sobs become more quiet. Suddenly there is a knock on the door.* TILLY *whispers:* Quiet! You're sleeping. Don't move. *He lies still. She stealthily goes to the door.* Who is it?

VOICE *also whispering:* Open the door....

TILLY: Who is it?

VOICE: Carl! TILLY *looks around at* ERNST *who raises himself on his hands.* TILLY *quickly opens the door, admits* CARL, *quickly closes door.*

TILLY: You're spotted! Get out quick!

CARL: Where?

53

TILLY: They must be right behind you. Watching the house. CARL *quickly goes over to the cot, touches* ERNST. *Starts for door again where* TILLY *has been listening.*

TILLY: They're coming! *Suddenly in a loud voice which* CARL *immediately takes up:* I'm telling you to get out. What's the matter—can't a respectable girl entertain her boy friend.

CARL: You made a date with me. *Simulates a drunkard.*

TILLY: You're a liar. Now get out before I call the police.

CARL: Didn't you say it! In the Park didn't you tell me to come tonight? Why, for two marks—— *Door is pushed open: two detectives in trench coats stand there.*

TILLY: My God! What's this, more customers?

DICK 1: Who's this?

TILLY: A fresh guy who pushed his way in. There's my boy friend, dead tired on the bed, fresh from the jug, and this garbage can won't let him rest.

CARL: Never mind that stuff! When I met her in the Kunzterplatz Tuesday she tells me to come up tonight. "I love you," she tells me.

TILLY: Yah, yah, yah!

DICK *comes in and looks around. Assistant blocks the door.* Is this your boy friend?

TILLY: Yeah. He's dead tired. He was——

DICK: All right, all right! *To* CARL: What do

you wanna start up with this alley cat for. You know they do it for anyone.

CARL: Sure.... But the next time I meet you in that same place at lunch time——

TILLY: Yah, yah, yah, yah.... Thanks, officer— a real man! DICK *pushes out protesting* CARL *and looks superciliously at* TILLY *as he closes door.* TILLY *stands in her place for a second, listens, then turns down to* ERNST.

ERNST: Did he get away?

TILLY: They believed every word. *Suddenly door pushed open.* DICK *stands there again.* What do you want? ...

DICK *advancing into room. Finally:* I forgot my glove, cutie. *Picks it up from table, goes back to door.* You wanna be careful. Better girls than you are in the jails.

TILLY: All right.

DICK: Lemme know if anyone makes trouble....

TILLY: All right.

DICK: Or if you're lonely some night.

TILLY: All right.

DICK *winking. Taps his chest:* A real man, me....

TILLY *first locking door:* Sleep, Ernst, sleep.... *But he is already asleep. She sits herself in window light in profile as daylight comes fuller in the window.*

BLACKOUT
Whistles

55

SCENE · VI

Comrades' Scene.
About a dozen party members
seated in a small locked room. The
SECRETARY *of the unit is finishing*
a report. CARL *sits downstage with*
back to audience. TILLY *is there.*
Also little BAUM *of the first scene.*
Sitting with a woman holding his
hand is a man with a fine looking
head, a famous theoretician, a shawl
over his shoulders, gray-haired—
STIEGLITZ. GUARD *at door.*

SECRETARY *reading:* Three new theater-of-action
groups have been formed in the last week. They
are now functioning regularly throughout the city.
Three thousand cheap jazz records have been dis-
tributed since the 10th. These each end in one of
our speeches. Since the first—— *Stops to admonish
a small man named* JULIUS, *who is wending his
way through some seated comrades.* Will the comrades kindly remain seated until the reports are
concluded.

JULIUS *who is revealed to be wearing only one
shoe:* I left my shoe in the corner. My foot is cold.

SECRETARY *continues:* Since the first we have
spent on Hitler joke books and leaflets the sum
of two hundred and ten marks. *Puts down report.*

I suggest that since we are all agreed on the accuracy of the report that we do not waste time but go ahead to other business. Will someone ask the question?

VARIOUS: The question, etc.

SECRETARY: All in favor will please assent in the usual manner.

ARNO: Just a minute. This seems to me to be in a way like a little steam rolling.

SECRETARY: Does the comrade have any suggestions in reference——

ARNO: No, but it seems——

OTHERS: Sit down, Arno.

ARNO: What about Comrade Tausig?

SECRETARY: Next.

ARNO: How was I supposed to know——

SECRETARY: All in favor. *The suggestion is passed. There is a slight respite. Improvisation.* We will now read the roll of honor.

COMRADE *gets up and reads:* "Unit 2026— "Killed in carrying out their proletarian duties, on the 3rd, Friedrich Meyers, Elsa Schorr. On the 12th, George Pfitzner. *In the background a woman suddenly sobs. She is comforted by another and soon stops.* Imprisoned or captured during this month, Paul Schnitzler, Ernst Tausig." *Sits.*

SECRETARY: This is not time for sentiment, but it would not be wrong to stop for one minute to remark upon the fine qualities of those valiant fighters who are now lost to our cause, some for-

ever. In the case of our slain fighters their merits
are known to all of us. In the case of Ernst Tausig
we must pause for serious consideration. It has been
proposed by the unit functionaries that his name
be added to the blacklist. But in accordance with
usual procedure we have brought this matter to
your attention in the hope of arriving at a wider
understanding of the case. Comrade Tilly Westermann.

TILLY *rises, wipes hands with small handkerchief:*
Since the reports on Ernst Tausig come from reliable sources we must give them strong credence.
Briefly he was first arrested in March. Three weeks
later he was released. CARL *turns around and looks
into the face of the audience.* At that time he
knew he was being followed. They were hoping he
would contact party members. This he positively
did not do. Four days later he was picked up again.
I saw him once after that in the hospital with his
brother. *Lapsing for one line into a less official,
less impersonal attitude:* I didn't recognize him. He
held my hand. . . . We wanted—— *Breaks off, stops
for a minute, resumes the impersonal tone:* It's no
secret to most of you that I am bearing his child.
This fact will seem to make for strong partiality
on my part. But I protest that because Ernst Tausig
was in a room when others identified prisoners is
no reason to assume that he has turned informer.
This is not the Tausig whom most of us have

known and worked with in the last four years or more.

BAUM: Right!

ARNO: How about when Mickle saw him with the police in the Herfheim Street raid? Maybe he was just knitting a muffler while he was sitting there next to the driver!

SECRETARY: The comrades will please ask permission for the floor. ARNO *raises his hand*. Comrade Arno?

ARNO *on his feet*: Personally, I'm sorry for Tausig. But who can take a chance nowadays? Even if he is not guilty, who can take a chance when the secret police have any connection with him?

SECRETARY: Please be more specific.

ARNO: I mean he must go on the blacklist. Every unit paper in the country must carry his name and description. For our purposes he is deadly, dangerous.

SECRETARY *recognizing Tilly*: Comrade Westermann?

TILLY: I can't disagree with what has just been said——

ARNO: I should say not!

TILLY: But will the chair permit me to read a small note I received from Ernst last week?

SECRETARY: Please read the note.

TILLY *reads*: "They are taking my life by the inch. Day and night they press me for an answer—

identify prisoners or be killed. I cannot last much longer. The terrible truth is they do not kill me. I am enclosing money which they handed over to me yesterday after forcing me to sit beside their chauffeur when they made a street raid. You may be sure I have kept my mouth shut. Love to Carl and you." *The man with one shoe comes over and looks at the note.*

SECRETARY: Before we decide the action in this case would any other comrade care to say something?

GIRL: Perhaps Comrade Stieglitz.

SECRETARY *looking in his direction*: I don't think.... *Companion of* STIEGLITZ *whispers to him. He nods.*

ZELDA: He says he will say a few words about the case.

SECRETARY: Comrade Stieglitz has just come back to us from three months in the Sonnenberg detention camp. *Pointedly.* I will ask you to listen carefully—to these few remarks from one of our leading theoreticians. *Small bandage on head. All wait. The imposing looking man gets up quietly and takes his place at the other side of the room, next to the* SECRETARY. *He looks around him gently, smiles softly at* TILLY.

STIEGLITZ: Always in such rare cases where there is a doubt as to the accused one's guilt it is the custom to be careful in consideration of the known facts. But a different face is placed on the matter in times of stress and danger. Often.... *He stops, thinks, continues.* Often the class struggle ... it seems to me ... it seems to me ... *He stops, a little puzzled, plays with fringe of shawl.* I was saying ... *Looks around helplessly. Walks over to his female companion.* Where are we, Zelda?

ZELDA: With friends, Benno.

STIEGLITZ: What was I saying?

ZELDA: Please sit down, Benno.

STIEGLITZ: Take me home, Zelda.... *Looks around helplessly.* Zelda....

SECRETARY *into the breach*: I think it would be best if he were home.

ZELDA: Yes. We're going, Benno. I have your hat.

STIEGLITZ: I'll hold your hand. Good-by, my friends, good-by. You must come to my house for breakfast. We have the sunniest breakfast room.... Yes.... *She leads him out. The door is locked behind him. She has been admonished first to be careful.* BAUM *blows his nose vigorously.*

BAUM. So have the devils broken that noble mind!!

SECRETARY: Comrades, now is no time for sentiment. This is the hour of steel, when—— No sentiment! *But he himself has to hide his tear-filled eyes. Presently controls himself.*

JULIUS: It's a pretty kettle of fish, I must say.

CARL *suddenly up:* I would like to say something in reference to my brother.

SECRETARY: Take the floor. *Piano and violin duo begin downstairs.*

CARL: Comrades, you are wondering where the music comes from. This is the very same house in which my brother and myself were born and raised. My uncle and his old friend, Seligmann are playing. The war, the revolution, the banishing of Jews from Germany have turned their poor old hearts to water. These days you will find them forever— the two of them playing their Mozart and Beethoven sonatas. The music they are playing now is Mozart, the andante of the C Major Sonata—C Major, my dear comrades, is a very wholesome beautiful key. You must excuse what may seem an irrelevant excursion into sentiment. But this is the first piece of Mozart my brother and I ever played together. When we came from school—I am surprised how fresh this dead life is in my memory—nineteen years back—but that's another story. *Now suddenly turning hard:* But Mozart— is there time for music today? What are we fighting for? I need not answer the question. Yes, it is brother against brother. Many a comrade has found with deep realization that he has no home, no brother—even no mothers or fathers! What must we do here? Is this what you asked me? We must expose this one brother wherever he is met. Whosoever looks in his face is to point the finger.

Children will jeer him in the darkest streets of his life! Yes, the brother, the erstwhile comrade cast out! There is no brother, no family, no deeper mother than the working class. Long live the struggle for true democracy! *He sits now.*

The music finishes before anyone speaks.

The vote is called for. All raise their hands in assent except TILLY. *She looks around at the others. One of the men is eating small nuts loudly. Her hand slowly comes up.*

FADEOUT

SCENE · VII

CARL's *room. Small. Only a door set up in center. In darkness we hear two typewriters. When lights fade up we see* CARL *and* TILLY *each at a typewriter. Typing.* TILLY *finally stops.*

TILLY: A few mistakes.

CARL *older:* No matter.

TILLY: My heart hurts. Hurt me all day.

CARL: Take care. Lie down before we go.

TILLY: I can't rest. *Comes down to him.*

TILLY: Carl, I want to ask you—are you ever afraid?

CARL: Sometimes.

TILLY: Now? Tell the truth.

CARL: Yes, if you want it. The place we're going to is swarming with S.S. men. We might never come out alive. I'm not so masculine that I won't admit I'm scared.

TILLY: All day I had this pain under the heart.

CARL: When will the baby be coming?

TILLY: A long time yet.

CARL *in a low voice:* What will you call him?

TILLY: If it's a girl, I don't know. If it's a boy....

CARL: Not *his* name.

64

TILLY *suddenly clutching him*: Tell me, how do you know? What makes you so sure?

CARL: There's proof—plenty!

TILLY: You believe it?

CARL: In the beginning I didn't. Maybe the brown shirts spread the tales themselves.

TILLY: They've done it before.

CARL: I don't say no. That's why I didn't believe a word I heard at first.

TILLY: Now you believe it.

CARL: Yes. Too many reliable comrades have checked on his activity.

TILLY: Maybe he's drugged. Maybe he walks in his sleep. You know—yes, you know—he would have found some way to do away with himself before he was forced to act as a spy. You know that! You know you do!

CARL: Don't tear my shirt. *Trying to jest.*

TILLY *persistently*: Answer the question!

CARL *finally, in a burst*: Goddamit, I say he's guilty!

TILLY: If he came here, broken in mind and body, would you refuse to see him? Can you stand there and tell me you wouldn't even listen to what he had to say?

CARL: To me he has nothing to say!

TILLY: He's your brother.

CARL: That won't sell a postage stamp!

TILLY: Suppose he knocks on the door this minute!

CARL: You're in love.

TILLY: Answer what I ask!

CARL: What makes you think you're the only one? Maybe I slept better at night the last two months. Maybe I cried myself to sleep some nights. This big blustering idiot wept like a girl. *Walks around.* Yes, yes, the whole thing funnels up in me like fever. My head'll bust a vein!

TILLY *catching herself:* We're talking too loud.

CARL *whispering, but with same intense flow:* Seeing him together at the hospital the last time—the picture follows me like a dog. I'm sick, I tell you I'm sick of the whole damn affair! *Sitting.* Perhaps we ought to change—do our work apart. This way, this is a secret eating thing between us. Each reminds the other.

TILLY: We'll talk about it tomorrow. I want to find a glass of milk before we start to work.

CARL: We'll get some on the corner.

TILLY: The baby has to eat. . . . *He gets her coat. Smiles at its shabbiness.*

CARL: Nothing is too good for the proletariat.

TILLY: I had a nice coat once. I had a mother. I had a father. I was a little girl with pigtails and her face scrubbed every morning. I was a good child. I believed in God. In summer I ate mulberries from our own tree. In late summer the ground was rotten where they fell. *Knock at the door.* Open the door. Don't ask who it is. It's Ernst, I know it is.

CARL *looks at her, puzzled.* TILLY *goes to open door. He stops her. Whispering:* Are you crazy?

TILLY: I know it's him.

CARL: Let the door alone.

VOICE *outside:* Carl....

CARL *covers door:* You can't let him in.

TILLY: You can't keep him out. *Waits.* He's waiting....

CARL: He'll go away.

TILLY: Maybe he's sick.

CARL: And the others in detention camps, they're not sick?

TILLY: You might be wrong.

CARL: Then better one mistake like this than a thousand arrests and murders.

VOICE *knocks without:* Carl....

TILLY: He won't leave. *After another knock.* Give me the key, Carl. CARL *looks at her. Puts key on table. Walks away. She opens door with it. Opens wide the door. There stands* ERNST. *Looks terrible. Wears a large velour hat, black, making his face look small. This man, sick, broken, alone, desperate, humble, something of amusement in him too. Has a handful of coins he plays with. Clothes are too big on him. Looks like a ghost.*

ERNST: Tilly....

TILLY: Come in, Ernst.

ERNST: May I...?

TILLY: Come in... *He does so.* CARL *on side, back turned.* TILLY *locks door. Retains key. She*

67

takes off his overcoat. He is revealed in a soiled shirt, tails out on one side. Takes off his hat while he plays with coins and looks at floor. His hair is streaked with white. He seems abstracted. Finally, becomes aware of room when coins drop out of his hand. He doesn't notice the coins.

ERNST: Tilly.... Let me.... *He slowly walks over to her, falls on his knees, kisses her hand. She draws her hand away.*

CARL *turning:* Stand up. ERNST *does so.* What do you want?

ERNST: I came——

CARL: To tell us lies.

TILLY: Let him talk. There are enough executioners in Germany without——

CARL: For the present I'm not used to one in my own room. For the present I——

ERNST *in a violent burst:* No. Stop it. No!

CARL: What is "no"? Mickle saw you with the police. Arno saw you in the court. You give the secret police information!

TILLY: They'll hear you in the street!

ERNST: Listen to me—— CARL *makes move for door.* ERNST *blocks it.* I came to have a talk.

CARL: Get out of my way.

ERNST: No!

CARL *pushes him away, throws him to floor. Finds door locked. Turns to* TILLY. *She puts the table between them:* Give me the key.

TILLY: No. CARL *looks at* ERNST. *Picks him up from floor. Sits aside.*

ERNST: It's all right—I understand—you don't want to listen. It's all right—I'll talk to myself. It's a habit now. I talk to myself on the street, frighten children—frighten myself. Don't listen to me. I'll talk to the chair. Here—— *Turns chair around, addresses it as to a person.* Mr. Chair! First, we understand the situation. Second, the charges are listed in our minds. TILLY, *out of pity and terror, removes the chair which he has been addressing very earnestly. Finally* ERNST *continues in a low, intense voice:* Now we must examine the living witness: what do you know of what happened? Who told you?

CARL *jumping up fiercely:* I won't listen to you.

ERNST *jumping up the same:* What am I asking of you? Pity? No! You must *know,* Tilly must know the accusations against me are untrue. I want you both to stand clear and proud in the world—not to think your brother and husband turned. . . .

CARL: I don't care for the personal issues.

ERNST: Then I care! For my son I care. He need never be ashamed to bear my name.

CARL: Every unit paper in the country screams out you're a rat.

ERNST: And they know?

CARL: You're damn right they know.

69

ERNST: When I was released from the barracks in General Pape street—did they know then?

CARL: That's four months back.

ERNST: They left me free that time.

CARL: Because you were supposed to lead them to the comrades.

ERNST: But I didn't.

CARL: Because you couldn't walk.

ERNST: So far so good, no?

TILLY: Yes. . . .

ERNST: Then they picked me up again. The whole thing started fresh—questioned day and night. No let-up. Swollen, bleeding, the hospital again. What good was I to them dead? Suddenly you fall—a bucket of water—they stand you up —the lash—dig your nails into the wall to remain standing.

CARL: When did you make up your mind to tell?

ERNST: Not yet!

TILLY: Not yet?

ERNST: They tie your feet, seat you with the driver on the round-ups. This makes you seem a guide for them.

CARL: But you never sent a message, not a warning.

ERNST: Two dozen. Intercepted. You don't believe it?

CARL: No.

70

ERNST: You're made to stand outside the court-room door where comrades pass.

CARL: We know all about it.

ERNST: Inside they say, "Don't make denials. Your former comrade told us everything." Some comrades believed that.

CARL: That explains the new clothes, money in your pocket?

ERNST: They dressed me up. That was the plan, to look like a paid stool pigeon. Then the first leaflet appears: "Ernst Tausig is a paid stool pigeon." Who printed them? Comrades? No, the Nazis. The comrades keep away. Out of the crowd some one hits me—it happens often. I turn around. Children hoot me on the street. All day and night the rank injustice freezes my heart to ice.

CARL: Why tell us, why——?

ERNST: They have a detective taking me home at nights. I live in his house. I can't understand. They did something to me. Sulphur is running in my veins. At night I wake up perspiring. My tongue is thick, my eyes won't open.

TILLY: Ernst, what can we do?

ERNST: Nothing, nothing. Only I want you to believe me. I must have some one believing me. I'm not a traitor. I'm not so far gone I don't understand the position I'm in. I see what you must do to me. Warn all party members against me. You can't know the truth. Yes, what is one person like me against the whole enslaved German working class? I know I must be cast away. But you two can believe me. Yes, officially you need not believe—but yourselves. Carl, don't look at me that way!

CARL: What is that?

ERNST: What?

CARL: Perfume? You're using perfume? Ladyfingers and whipped cream for breakfast.

ERNST: No, you see how it was. They gave me money. It falls out of my hands. My mind wanders like smoke. I passed the store the other day and it was in the window. Perfumed soap. I bought some. A man must have something. It smells like flowers. *Sits with abstracted quality. Finally says, after* CARL *removes leaflets on table from his sight:* Five weeks ago—I think it was the 8th of last month—I don't remember—the day we had the thunder shower—the hand was badly infected—it seems I knocked it against the wall or something— the 9th or 10th—they amputated it. We had that fine surgeon, D. B. Kellner. *There is a luminous full pause. Yes, his hand has been removed and all this time he kept the stump in a pocket. Does not take it out now either.* TILLY, *unbearably moved, comes to him. He refuses her touch. Jumps up.* Don't touch me. No, it isn't so easy. Three months—it's not so easy. That's why I'm telling you. *You must know everything!* Last night I sat in my room and it came to me. I was thinking that when I went there the next day I would tell them everything. *Laughs and changes voice to a whisper.* Do you know what you must do? I brought the whole thing with me. A gun, cleaned, oiled. This morning I did it. With one hand it isn't easy. Kill me!

CARL: What?

ENRST: Take the gun. Carl, you loved me once. Kill me. One day more and I'll stand there like an idiot identifying prisoners for them. I know so many. In all honor and courage you must pull the little trigger. I brought the money. Put it in the fighting fund. Maybe tell a few comrades the truth.

CARL: It is the truth?

ERNST: Yes.

TILLY: There must be no talk of dying.

ERNST: For me there's one thing, Tilly—nothing is left to do. Carl——?

CARL: They've killed you already.

ERNST: That's right. But you're alive. Other comrades are working. The day is coming and I'll be in the final result. That right can't be denied me. In that dizzy dazzling structure some part of me is built. You must understand. Take the gun, Carl.

CARL *drawing hand away:* I won't do it.

ERNST: I couldn't do it myself. There isn't enough strength left.... Tilly, no tears! *Smiles wearily.* Such bourgeois traits in a worker ... What is your answer, Carl?

73

CARL: That is what you must do. Do it yourself. Before you turn idiot. When you do that the world will know you were innocent. They'll see you came voluntarily, that. . . . *Suddenly:* Who am I to sit in judgment?

ERNST: These guns are complicated pieces of machinery. *Has picked it up.* Our Germans make them like works of art. *Weighs the gun in his hand.* Tilly, Carl, our agony is real. But we live in the joy of a great coming people! The animal kingdom is past. Day must follow the night. Now we are ready: we have been steeled in a terrible fire, but soon all the desolate places of the world must flourish with human genius. Brothers will live in the soviets of the world! Yes, a world of security and freedom is waiting for all mankind! *Looks at them both deeply. Walks to door to room L.* Do your work, Comrades. *Exits.*

TILLY *for a moment stands still. Then starts for room.* CARL *stops her:* Carl, stop him, stop him. CARL *holds her back.*

CARL: Let him die. . . .

TILLY: Carl. . . . *Shot heard within.*

CARL: Let him live. . . .

SLOW CURTAIN